GeetaSaptadashi

17 Life Matters As I Have Perceived

Rani Acharya

For permissions, contact:

rani.acharya@outlook.com

ISBN: **978-93-340-5940-3**

Printed and bound in India by Amazon.com

Offered unto the Divine feet of

Shri Krishn

Contents

PREFACE

Life is a journey of endless questions, each one a doorway to deeper understanding. Over the years, I have found myself standing at the crossroads of such questions, grappling with the mysteries of existence, purpose, and the unseen forces that shape our lives. These inquiries have often felt overwhelming, like waves crashing against the shores of my mind, demanding answers that seem just out of reach.

In my search for clarity, the timeless teachings of Indian scriptures, particularly the Bhagavad Geeta, have been a guiding light. They have not only shaped my values but also offered profound insights into the challenges we face in modern life. What fascinates me most is how these ancient verses, written millennia ago, remain deeply relevant in a world that has changed so much.

From a young age, I was drawn to the wisdom of these texts, captivated by their depth and universality. As I delved deeper into their teachings, I realized that their truths extend far beyond rituals and traditions. They address the core of human existence - our struggles, desires, fears, and hopes.

This book is my humble attempt to bridge the timeless wisdom of the Bhagavad Geeta with the questions and dilemmas of today. It is a reflection of my journey - a quest to make sense of life's complexities through the lens of this sacred scripture. Each chapter draws from its verses to offer insights that speak to the challenges faced by young individuals, parents, and seekers alike, weaving together ancient teachings with modern experiences.

I invite you to embark on this exploration with me, not as a reader, but as a fellow traveler. May this book serve as a companion on your path, inspiring you to look within and discover answers to your own questions. Together, let us uncover the relevance of the eternal truths that have stood the test of time.

May these words inspire a sense of clarity, devotion, and inner peace as you turn each page.

ANXIETY

Q1. Is Anxiety just a trend in this generation and how to overcome it if suffering?

Anxiety, it seems, is not a new companion; it has walked with humanity for centuries. Even in the distant past, during the Dwapara Yuga over 5,000 years ago, it found its way into the minds of those who lived. Arjun, the valiant warrior, standing at the precipice of Kurukshetra battle, was consumed by an overwhelming inner storm - fear, doubt, and confusion clouding his mind. His struggle on that sacred battlefield, far beyond mere physical combat, was a reflection of the emotional battles we all face at some point in our lives. His strength and courage were not enough to shield him from the weight of his inner turmoil. This timeless moment serves as a deep reminder: no matter how strong, accomplished, or revered we may be, the human experience is vulnerable to anxiety.

Have you ever felt your mind spiraling into a whirlwind of "what-ifs," painting vivid pictures of scenarios that may never come to pass? In the ceaseless rush of today's world, anxiety has quietly slipped into the lives of countless people, irrespective of age and circumstance. It's as pervasive as the air we breathe, yet it leaves an invisible burden on our hearts - pressing, persistent, and deeply personal.

If I were to encapsulate anxiety in just two words, I would call it "baseless thinking." It's a poignant description of how our thoughts can become untethered from reality, spinning tales of fear and doubt that have no foundation. We allow these imagined worries to grow, feeding them with attention and emotion until they overshadow the simplicity of the present moment.

The paradox is striking: much of what keeps us awake at night could dissolve with a single shift in focus, a gentle reminder to be here now. Yet, instead of untangling these threads of thoughts, we weave them tighter - analyzing, overanalyzing, and amplifying what was never as complex as it seemed. In doing so, we lose sight of the beauty and clarity that comes with living fully in the present, free from the chains of our own making.

Overanalysis often stems from a profound and hidden fear - a fear that subtly whispers in our minds, urging us to examine every possible outcome of a situation, whether good or bad. This fear becomes a relentless companion, driving us to mentally rehearse scenarios that may never come to pass. Anxiety thrives in these moments, particularly when our thoughts veer toward the negative, pulling us away from the beauty and peace of the present.

In today's fast-paced world, anxiety has surged alongside

our deepening entanglement with the material and our waning connection to the spiritual. We place immense weight on the outcomes of our actions, clinging to them as if our worth depends solely on success or failure. This attachment, this incessant need to control and foresee, tightens the grip of anxiety on our hearts and minds.

But imagine, just for a moment, the peace that comes from letting go - from releasing the need to dictate every detail of life's unfolding. If we could loosen our attachment to results, we might uncover not only a pathway to inner calm but also a solution to countless other struggles. In letting go, there lies the promise of freedom - a quiet antidote to the chaos within.

In the grand epic of the Mahabharata, Arjun's journey offers a deeply emotional lens into the torment of inner conflict. A warrior celebrated for his unmatched valor and precision, Arjun found himself immobilized not by the strength of his enemies but by the weight of his own heart (Reddy 2012). Standing on the battlefield of Kurukshetra, his bow trembled, and his vision blurred - not with fear of death, but with the agonizing dilemma of fighting his own blood.

In that moment of great vulnerability, the injustices he had endured seemed to fade into the background. The betrayal of the Kauravas, the humiliation of Draupadi, and the unyielding arrogance of Duryodhan - all were eclipsed by a deeper fear: the pain of severing ties with those he still called family. Victory, once his ultimate goal, now seemed a cruel illusion, as it demanded a price he wasn't sure he could pay. The thought of triumph felt hollow, for it meant standing amidst the ruins of relationships and memories that once brought him comfort.

Arjun's heart wrestled with the chaos before him - love clashing with duty, justice entangled with despair. His spirit, so accustomed to the rhythm of battle, faltered in the face of this emotional storm, revealing a poignant truth: even the strongest among us can be unmoored when our values and emotions collide.

तत्रापश्यत्स्थितान् पार्थ: पितृनथ पितामहान्।
आचार्यान्मातुलान्भ्रातृन्पुत्रान्पौत्रान्सखींस्तथा।
श्रशुरान्सुहृदश्षेव सेनयोरु भयोरपि॥ 1.26

{There Arjun could see, within the midst of the armies of both parties, his fathers, grandfathers, teachers, maternal uncles, brothers, sons, grandsons, friends, and also his fathers-in-law and well-wishers.}

तान्समीक्ष्य स कौन्तेय: सर्वान्बन्धूनवस्थितान्।
कृपया परयाविष्टो विषीदन्निदमब्रवीत्॥ 1.27

{When the son of Kunti, Arjun, saw all these different grades of friends and relatives, he became overwhelmed with compassion and spoke thus.}

दृष्ट्वेमं स्वजनं कृष्ण युयुत्सुं समुपस्थितम्।
सीदन्ति मम गात्राणि मुखं च परिशुष्यति॥ 1.28

{Arjun said: My dear Krishn, seeing my friends and relatives present before me in such a fighting spirit, I feel the limbs of my body quivering and my mouth drying up.}

वेपथुश्च शरीरे मे रोमहर्षश्च जायते।
गाण्डीवं स्रंसते हस्तात्त्वक्चैव परिदह्यते॥ 1.29

{My whole body is trembling, my hair is standing on end, my bow Gandiv is slipping from my hand, and my skin is burning.}

न च शक्नोम्यवस्थातुं भ्रमतीव च मे मनः।
निमित्तानि च पश्यामि विपरीतानि केशव॥ 1.30

{I am now unable to stand here any longer. I am forgetting myself, and my mind is reeling. I see only causes of misfortune, O Krishn, killer of the Kesi demon.}

In the depths of despair, Arjun found himself at a crossroads, overwhelmed by self-doubt and fear. In this vulnerable moment, he was blessed to have the divine presence of Krishn by his side - a beacon of wisdom and unwavering support. Krishn, with infinite patience, offered clarity and guidance through the teachings of the Bhagavad Geeta. Yet, these teachings were never meant for Arjun alone. They transcend time and space, echoing across generations, offering insight to all who seek them.

Krishn understood that even a hero as resolute as Arjun could falter when gripped by anxiety. Arjun's turmoil revealed a universal truth: no one is immune to the weight of doubt, nor to the pull of attachment and fear of failure. Krishn's foresight extended beyond the battlefield of Kurukshetra; he envisioned a future where humanity, distanced from spiritual grounding, would struggle even more profoundly.

Today, this disconnection from spirituality, compounded by our relentless fixation on results, has made enduring life's challenges feel like steering a ship through a storm without a compass. It is here that the Bhagavad Geeta shines as an eternal guide - a reservoir of timeless wisdom that gently reminds us how to align our actions with purpose, find strength in surrender, and lead a life of balance, fulfillment, and inner peace.

From Arjun's journey, we uncover valuable lessons that deeply resonate with our struggles against anxiety. In the battlefield of life, Krishn's words gently remind us that the root of this turmoil often lies in the heart's fragility. It is the wavering strength of our inner self, burdened by doubts and fears, that fuels this unease. Just as Arjun hesitated before his challenges, we too falter, but within his story lies a timeless truth - our hearts are capable of courage, if only we allow wisdom to guide us through the storm.

क्लैब्यं मा सम गमः पार्थ नेतत्त्वय्युपपद्यते।
क्षुद्रे हृदयदौर्बल्यं त्यक्त्वोत्तिष्ठ परन्तप॥ 2.3

{O son of Prtha, do not yield to this degrading impotence. It does not befit you. Give up such petty weakness of heart and arise, O chastiser of the enemy.}

To cope with anxiety, we can embrace three essential steps before responding to stressful situations, each offering a gentle yet powerful way to regain control over our emotions.

The first step is to *stop*. In moments of anxiety, when our minds race like a wild stallion, the thought of halting can feel overwhelming. It's as if we're trying to tame an unruly beast. But even the briefest pause - just five seconds - can create a shift, offering a small, quiet space to interrupt the chaos. This tiny pause prevents us from spiraling into unnecessary worry and gives us a chance to re-center ourselves.

The second step is to *breathe.* Though breathing is a natural function, we often forget to truly feel it. In times of stress, we tend to breathe shallowly, restricting the flow of calm. By consciously inhaling deeply, filling our lungs and then releasing, we create a soothing rhythm. This simple act of breathing replenishes both body and mind, grounding us in the present moment and calming the storm within. The oxygen we take in becomes nourishment for our emotions, offering a quiet refuge from the turbulence of our thoughts (Annual Review of Neuroscience).

The final step is to *reflect.* When we take a step back from the immediate pressure of a situation, we gain distance and perspective. This broader view helps us assess whether our emotional response is truly necessary or if it's born from overreaction. In this space of reflection, we often discover that the anxiety we once felt begins to fade. Our minds clear, and what seemed overwhelming moments before becomes manageable. Reflecting allows us to break free from the trap of overthinking, empowering us to approach challenges with clarity and calmness.

By practicing these three steps – *stop, breathe, reflect* – we shift from reaction to reflection, from chaos to clarity. We learn to meet anxiety not with fear or resistance, but with understanding, creating space for peace in the midst of life's storms.

Through personal experience, I have come to understand the power of this method. In moments of emotional turmoil, I often made decisions I later regretted, driven by the intensity of the situation. But once I began to embrace this technique, everything began to shift. At first, taking a pause during a heated argument felt unnatural, almost impossible and awkward. Yet, as time went on, I experienced the immense peace it brought. The discomfort was temporary, but the clarity and emotional stability it afforded me were priceless.

This method reminds me of a beautiful story from the life of Buddha, one that speaks to the deep power of patience and stillness. There was a time when Buddha sent one of his disciples to fetch water from a nearby river. Upon reaching the river, the disciple was disheartened to find the water thick with mud, making it impossible to collect. He returned, empty-handed, only to be instructed by Buddha to try again later. The disciple followed the instruction, and once again, the river greeted him with murky water. This pattern repeated three times - each time, the water was too polluted to use. Finally, after allowing time to pass, the disciple arrived at the river once more, and to his astonishment, the water was now clear and pure. He eagerly filled his pot and hurried back to Buddha. When Buddha asked him if he had done anything to purify the water, the disciple humbly replied that he had not. Buddha then explained with a calm smile that just as the mud in the river settled over time, so too can the turbulence within our minds settle if we give it the time and space it needs.

This story beautifully illustrates how, in moments of inner chaos and confusion, sometimes all we need is patience. We must allow our thoughts, our emotions, our very selves, the gift of rest. Only then can the clarity and peace we long for emerge. When we deny our minds this much-needed stillness, we risk becoming disconnected from our true selves, losing touch with the very essence of our humanity. Allowing time for quiet reflection is not just a luxury, but a necessary practice for our mental well-being, one that restores the soul and helps us rediscover our peace.

Yet, in the midst of his deepest despair, there came a voice of calm - Krishn's words, timeless in their wisdom, whispered a powerful truth: even in our most difficult, bewildering moments, we are never truly alone. There is a wellspring of strength and clarity within us, waiting to be tapped. Krishn's teachings continue to resonate through the ages, offering solace to all who face the storms within. His wisdom reminds us that no darkness is everlasting and that peace, though elusive at times, is always within reach.

In a world where anxiety often feels like an unavoidable companion, ancient wisdom reminds us that we hold the power to reclaim peace within. The Bhagavad Geeta reveals that even the greatest warriors, like Arjun, can feel lost when burdened by fear and overwhelming emotions. In those moments of darkness, the true strength is not in fighting the storm, but in learning to move through it with a calm heart.

The key lies in loosening our grip on the outcomes we so desperately seek and instead, nurturing a quiet connection to our deeper, spiritual selves. When we find this balance, anxiety loses its hold, and we can move forward with a steadier heart.

Each time we pause, allowing our breath to fill the air around us, and when we take a moment to reflect, we are, in essence, weaving threads of peace and balance into our lives. It's in these quiet moments that we begin to align ourselves with stillness, shedding the noise that clouds our hearts. For, in truth, the greatest struggle isn't one of external forces, but the unseen battle that rages within us, in the corners of our minds. It's there, in the depths of our thoughts and emotions, where the real test lies, asking us to find serenity amidst the storm. As, in the game of life, the mind is the controller; those who master it emerge as true victors. Remember, we are the masters of our minds, not its servants.

FAITH

Q.2. Why does our faith in God tremble when we are in the shattering state of our life?

Life has a way of testing us in the most unexpected ways, often plunging us into circumstances that leave us feeling lost and helpless. In these moments of turmoil, doubt creeps in, clouding our ability to see the way forward. For those with spiritual inclinations, the instinct is often to turn to God - to seek His shelter and find solace in His presence. Yet, even as we bow our heads in prayer, our hearts may still tremble, uncertain of the outcome.

This brings us to a deeply personal and thought-provoking question: If we claim to believe in God, why does our faith falter during life's storms? Why do we struggle to trust in His divine plan when we need it the most? The answer lies not in God's power but in the fragility of our faith. Perhaps our fear of things going against our desires outweighs our trust in His ability to guide us. Or perhaps, despite our declarations of faith, we have never truly cultivated a deep and unwavering connection with Him.

It's a humbling realization. We often place more belief in the power of our fears than in the infinite grace of the Almighty. Our minds are quick to spiral into negative thoughts, weaving worst-case scenarios that eclipse the light of God's love and protection. This isn't because God has turned away from us; it's because we've allowed the weight of our own doubts to obscure His presence. The problem lies not with Him but within us - our inability to fully trust, to surrender, and to recognize His boundless compassion and strength.

Faith in God, like any relationship, requires nurturing. It's not enough to simply believe in the existence of God; we must actively seek to know Him, to understand His nature, and to build a bond so profound that even the fiercest storms cannot shake it. Faith is not the absence of fear but the courage to trust in God's wisdom even when the path ahead seems uncertain.

To strengthen this trust, we must draw closer to Him - not just in moments of despair but in every moment of our lives. The scriptures offer us a powerful gateway to this connection. They reveal God as He truly is - a loving protector, a wise guide, and a constant source of strength. When we immerse ourselves in these teachings, we begin to see life through His lens, recognizing that even our struggles are laced with purpose and grace.

Faith is a journey, not a destination. The more we open our hearts to God, the more we realize that He has been with us all along, waiting patiently for us to trust Him. And as we take steps to deepen this bond - through prayer, scripture, and reflection - we discover a peace that fear can no longer overshadow. In knowing Him, we learn to trust Him, and in trusting Him, we find the courage to face anything life brings our way.

श्रद्धावल्लभते ज्ञानं तत्परः संयतेन्द्रियः।

ज्ञानं लब्ध्वा परां शान्तिमचिरेणाधिगच्छति॥ 4.39

{A faithful man, dedicated to transcendental knowledge and controlling his senses, is eligible to achieve such wisdom. Once attained, he quickly reaches supreme spiritual peace.}

अज्ञश्चाश्रद्दधानश्च संशयात्मा विनश्यति।

नायं लोकोऽस्ति न परो न सुखं संशयात्मनः॥ 4.40

{But ignorant and faithless individuals, who doubt the revealed scriptures, do not attain God-consciousness; they fall. For those who doubt, there is no happiness in this world or the next.}

At this moment, we stand at a crucial crossroads, a point where our next step has the power to shape not just the course of our lives, but the essence of who we are. On one side lies a path of faith - a chance to deepen our connection with the divine, to allow our understanding of God to blossom into something steady, beautiful, and transformative. This path invites us to open our hearts fully, to surrender the weight of our doubts, and to trust in a presence greater than ourselves. It's a journey that teaches us to see life through eyes of wonder and gratitude, to embrace the sacred in every moment, and to find comfort in the knowledge that we are never truly alone.

On the other side, however, is a path that feels safer but is infinitely more isolating. It is the choice to close ourselves off, to turn away from the whispers of awe and divinity that echo within us. This path is paved with skepticism and fear - a refusal to lean into the unknown, a resistance to the possibility of something greater guiding our steps. It's a path that robs us of the chance to feel God's gentle presence in our lives, to witness the miracles hidden in the mundane, and to experience the peace that only faith can offer.

And here we are, standing on the threshold, faced with a decision that will resonate far beyond this moment. There is no middle ground; we either embrace the light of faith or retreat into the shadows of uncertainty. The choice is deeply personal, yet its impact flows through every facet of our existence. It shapes how we face challenges, how we find meaning, and how we love ourselves and others.

To choose faith is to take a leap into the unknown, trusting that the net will appear, woven by the hands of the loving God. It is not the absence of fear, but the courage to move forward despite it. To choose otherwise is to risk losing touch with the divine thread that connects us all, leaving us to navigate life with only our limited vision and fragile strength.

This moment calls for courage, for honesty with ourselves, and for a willingness to open the door to grace. The choice is ours - and it is one that will echo within us, shaping not just our path but the depth of our souls.

Faith, at its core, is shaped by the environment we grow

up in. When a child grows up in a home where spirituality is at the center, surrounded by family members who live by sacred teachings and moral values, that sense of connection often stays with them into adulthood. Such an upbringing tends to foster a deep sense of trust in something greater than oneself. This trust becomes a steady anchor through life's challenges, not because of blind belief, but because the foundation of their spiritual understanding was built on something real, something that offers direction and meaning amidst the unpredictability of life.

On the other hand, a child brought up in an environment where the concept of a higher power is either non-existent or dismissed may struggle to see beyond their own perspective. Without the comforting guidance of spiritual belief or the lessons passed down through generations, they might grow up with a sense of independence that feels isolating at times. Their view of the world could become limited to what they can manage or control, focusing only on what they can touch, rather than feeling the pull of something greater that might offer them peace, purpose, or understanding beyond their immediate reach. This absence of spiritual perspective may leave them unaware of a deeper connection that binds all things, making it harder to surrender to the idea that there's more at play than what meets the eye.

When the theist faces life's challenges in adulthood, they hold onto an unwavering hope, rooted in the belief that a higher power is always by their side. Even in moments when the weight of the world seems unbearable, and the road ahead feels uncertain, they find comfort in the idea that they are not alone. Their mind remains anchored in a quiet hope, as they hold firm to the understanding that God's presence in their life is a constant, unshakable force.

Though reality may not unfold as they had envisioned, there is a profound sense of trust that the twists and turns they face are not random. Instead, they believe these moments are part of a much larger, divine plan - a plan crafted by a power whose wisdom transcends their own. The theist knows that God sees what they cannot, understanding a grander narrative that stretches beyond time and space, connecting the dots in ways they may never fully comprehend. It's a surrender to something greater, where faith isn't just a belief but a steady companion that provides comfort, even when the journey ahead seems unclear.

While, an atheist may begin life with a fierce sense of determination, confident in their own ability to face whatever comes their way rooted in their will power. They might feel invincible at first, fueled by the belief that their strength, intellect, and efforts are enough to overcome any obstacle. However, as life relentlessly throws its challenges at them, they may eventually start to feel the strain. The hope that once propelled them forward begins to fade, leaving in its place a crushing sense of helplessness. It's as if the world they had carefully built around their own strength begins to unravel. The belief that they control every aspect of their fate - their success, their failures - slowly turns into a heavy burden.

When things don't unfold as they had envisioned, their

confidence begins to crack. The weight of their own expectations becomes unbearable, and the hope they once held so firmly begins to crumble. Beneath the surface of their struggle lies a deep-seated belief that they are the sole architects of their life's journey. This mindset often leads to a painful realization: that when the plans they worked so hard to create fall apart, there is no safety net, no guiding force beyond their own willpower to help them regain balance.

At the heart of this experience is a sense of isolation - an inability to perceive that life may not only be about their individual efforts, but could also be about something greater than their understanding. It's the inability to recognize the existence of forces beyond their control, forces that might shape the course of their life in ways they could never have predicted. This absence of awareness can leave them feeling helpless and insignificant, trapped within the confines of their own limited perspective.

This scenario highlights the importance of becoming a seeker, someone who dares to ask the deep and meaningful questions that stir the soul. Questions like: How does the universe truly work? Is there a higher force, a guiding hand, shaping the course of our lives? Am I, in the end, responsible for everything I experience? Does magic, in its truest sense, exist in the world around us? It's ignorance, that silent thief, that rattles our faith and leaves us uncertain. But when we begin to open our hearts and minds to the ways in which God's power touches every corner of our lives, doubt begins to fade. For misconception is a fog, truth is a glow.

बुद्धिर्ज्ञानमसंमोहः क्षमा सत्यं दमः शमः।

सुखं दुःखं भवोऽभावो भयं चाभयमेव च॥ 10.4

अहिंसा समता तुष्टिस्तपो दानं यशोऽयशः।

भवन्ति भावा भूतानां मत्त एव पृथग्विधाः॥ 10.5

{Intelligence, knowledge, freedom from doubt and delusion, forgiveness, truthfulness, control of the senses, control of the mind, happiness and distress, birth and death, fear and fearlessness, nonviolence, equanimity, satisfaction, austerity, charity, fame and infamy - all these various qualities in living beings are created by Me alone.}

As Krishn assures us, every emotion - whether born from trust or doubt - finds its source in Him. This truth, however, becomes clear only when we step beyond the boundaries of our human limitations and open ourselves to a deeper understanding. When we come to realize this, we see that our positive qualities are not merely personal achievements but gifts of divine grace. And in moments when we feel the absence of these qualities, it's a call to realign ourselves with what is righteous and true.

Emotions, at their core, are a reflection of divine creation. Just as an artist imbues a masterpiece with intention, God infuses every emotion with purpose. And, as the artist evaluates their work, ensuring each brushstroke aligns with their vision, God, too, tests these emotions. This process is not cruel or arbitrary, but rather a means of shaping and refining what is inherently good. Much like a programmer who designs software and then thoroughly examines it for flaws, God leads us through experiences that challenge our hearts, encouraging us to grow and reveal our true selves. These trials are not meant to break us but to help us understand the depth of our strength, resilience, and compassion. Through every hardship, the rawness of our emotions is revealed, and in those moments, we are given the opportunity to reconnect with our essence, allowing us to emerge more whole and aware of the beauty within.

I came across a quote recently that truly stuck with me: "Both faith and fear demand that you believe in something you cannot see." It's so simple, yet so deeply real. In our lives, we are constantly faced with moments that test our belief in what we can't physically touch or understand. Whether we rise to meet these challenges or fall under their weight is completely up to us.

What stands out to me most is the idea that the strength of our faith is tied to how close we are to God. Faith is what fills temples with people, all united by a quiet trust in something greater than themselves. But the foundation of that faith must be strong enough to accept that God's plan for us may not always match what we think we want. There are times when we may struggle, question, or feel lost, but true faith asks us to trust that everything happening, even the hard moments, is part of a bigger picture - one that is ultimately for our good.

DEVOTION

Q3. Why am I not getting the results of my prayers?

As children, the memory of visiting temples with our parents is etched in our hearts like a cherished keepsake. In those tender years, we were gently guided to bow our heads and press our palms together in prayer before the deity. It was a simple act, one we embraced with the purest faith, not questioning but trusting wholeheartedly.

With time, as we grew and life revealed its layers, the meaning of prayer began to unfold in ways we hadn't anticipated. What started as a ritual slowly became a space where our hearts whispered their deepest wishes. As little ones, our prayers were delightfully innocent - hoping for a favorite toy or a piece of chocolate that would brighten our day.

As school life beckoned, our desires took a different shape. We prayed with trembling hearts for good grades, clutching onto faith before every exam. Then came the storm of teenage years, a time when prayers often carried the weight of fragile emotions - seeking the courage to confess a crush, longing for the bond of love, or simply hoping to clear the hurdles of semester exams.

Each phase of life brought a different shade to our prayers, reflecting the journey of our hearts and the dreams we dared to hold close. As the days go by, there are moments when the spark of prayer seems to fade. It feels as though the once-vivid connection to the divine has grown distant, leaving us questioning if God is truly listening. Sometimes, we resign ourselves to this feeling, believing it to be our destined reality. At other times, frustration takes over, and we silently accuse God of turning away from our pain. In our quiet despair, we might even begin to doubt the purpose of prayer itself, forgetting the countless instances when our heartfelt cries were met with answers.

But have we ever stopped to truly reflect on why this shift occurs? This thought weighed on my heart and lingered in my mind, pulling me toward a path of introspection. What had changed - the nature of prayer, or something within me? These questions became my companions as I embarked on a deeper exploration of my own faith and its delicate dance with life's uncertainties.

As I delve into the memories of my childhood, I find myself transported to a time when my father gently guided me through the sacred act of prayer. With his calm and steady hands, he taught me to press my palms together, bow my head before the divine, and offer a silent, heartfelt gratitude for the blessings I had received. He emphasized humility in seeking forgiveness for my mistakes - whether they arose from ignorance or intention. Asking for anything, however, was never part of our prayers. "God already knows what you need," he would remind me with a reassuring smile. And I believed him. My young heart felt content, as though an unseen force had carefully laid out everything I could ever require, even if I lacked the wisdom to see it.

But as the years passed and I grew older, innocence gave way to longing. My prayers began to carry small wishes - requests for fleeting comforts. I asked for better grades, for forgiveness when my harsh words wounded someone unintentionally, or for a quick end to the ache of a stomach ache. These wishes, tender and unassuming, often found answers, further affirming my faith in the divine presence that seemed so close, so personal.

Yet now, as I reflect on recent years, I sense a change. The quiet clarity of divine guidance, once as steady as a gentle breeze, feels distant, almost obscured. My prayers, though still earnest, seem to drift unanswered, leaving me to wonder if perhaps the divine silence holds lessons I am not yet ready to hear.

It slowly became clear to me that in my longing to ask God for what I desired, I had lost sight of the true meaning of prayer - a lesson my father had lovingly passed down to me. Prayer wasn't meant to be a plea or a demand; it was meant to be a bridge, a way to connect deeply with the divine. And yet, despite this realization, a part of me remained restless. Doubts churned within me, refusing to settle, as if my heart was at war with itself, searching for answers that I wasn't ready to accept. This inner struggle felt like a storm I couldn't calm, a whisper I couldn't ignore. I knew I had to confront it, to find clarity and peace, but the path forward felt uncertain, and the weight of my emotions was too much to bear.

One evening, on my visit to an ISKON temple I sought guidance from prabhuji (monk). My heart was heavy with doubt, and I needed answers that could bring clarity to my restless mind. I poured my thoughts and uncertainties into the air, and after listening patiently, the monk looked at me with gentle eyes and said, "Child, you are correct." His words felt like a soothing balm, comforting me in a way I hadn't expected. A smile tugged at my lips, the warmth of his affirmation filling me with a quiet sense of peace, as though I had just found a gentle hand to hold in my confusion.

He went on to speak, his voice calm yet imbued with the weight of wisdom. "There is a way to pray," he said, his words simple, yet they carried an undeniable truth. "It is not just about asking, but about how we approach the Divine." He smiled softly, continuing, "We begin by greeting God, much like we would greet a dear relative or a close friend - warmly, with respect, and with an open heart. Then, we offer our praises, acknowledging all the blessings He has granted us, the countless gifts that often go unnoticed. It is only after this, once our hearts are full of gratitude, that we can share our desires, if any. But even then, we must leave them in His hands, trusting that He knows what is best for us, even when we cannot see it ourselves."

His words lingered with me, stirring something deep within, as though they were not just a lesson on prayer but a guide to surrender and trust, a reminder of the beauty in gratitude.

When we allow ourselves to fully embrace the beauty and magnificence of the divine, something deep within us stirs, and we find ourselves drawn into a quiet peace. In these precious moments, it's as if the weight of the world lifts, and all the distractions that once seemed so important fade away. Our hearts, once filled with longing for material things, begin to shift. The desires that once defined us become distant echoes, replaced by a yearning for something pure and lasting: a connection with the divine. Our prayers no longer revolve around the things we think we need, but instead, they become a humble plea for closeness, for oneness with the Divine, where true fulfillment resides.

मच्चित्ता मद्गतप्राणा बोधयन्तः परस्परम्।

कथयन्तश्च मां नित्यं तुष्यन्ति च रमन्ति च॥ 10.9

{The thoughts of My pure devotees dwell in Me, their lives are fully devoted to My service, and they derive great satisfaction and joy from always enlightening one another and conversing about Me.}

Here, I found the answer I had been searching for. There was a time in my life when I became so consumed by the desire for my prayers to be answered that I forgot the true essence of what I had learned as a child. I was so caught up in asking for things - hoping, wishing, pleading - that I lost sight of something far more important. In all my yearning, I had forgotten to see God as a companion, a friend, someone I could converse with, not just someone to turn to for favors. In my silent desperation, I had turned Him into a distant figure instead of the close, caring presence He had always been.

Similarly, in the *Upanishads*, there is a concept of *Ishvara* (the supreme divine) knowing our deepest needs and desires, but responding according to what is best for us in our spiritual journey. In the *Chandogya Upanishad*, it is said:

यस्यां समक्षं यजते स यं यत्सं ज्ञानम्।

स बन्धनं हित्वा मुक्त्यं स्वात्मनं प्रतिष्ठते॥ 7.23॥

{The divine is the self within all beings, and it is through understanding the self that we truly understand all that we need.}

This teaches us that the answers to our prayers are often wrapped in the lessons we are meant to learn along the way. The true result of prayer may not always be immediate or tangible, but it leads us toward deeper self-awareness, trust, and ultimately, a more fulfilling connection with the divine.

To better understand this, imagine two close friends, Shreya and Anaya. Shreya, with her dreams of a life filled with luxury, comes from a humble, middle-class family. She yearns for the lavish experiences she sees others enjoying, but her reality doesn't afford her that. On the other hand, Anaya comes from a family of wealth and privilege. She's never had to worry about money and has access to all the beautiful things that Shreya can only dream of.

Whenever a fancy event comes up that Shreya wants to attend, she's quick to shower Anaya with compliments, praising her style and grace, knowing well that Anaya's life is everything she longs for. Anaya, with her kind and generous heart, always responds with warmth, her smile lighting up the room. After basking in the glow of the compliments, Shreya gently asks if she could borrow a dress from Anaya's exquisite closet.

Anaya, feeling touched by the admiration and eager to please her friend, not only lends her the dress but also adds matching jewelry, making sure Shreya feels nothing less than a princess. She does all this with a heart full of generosity, believing that her friend's happiness is just as important as her own. The exchange, though rooted in simplicity, speaks volumes about the deeper layers of friendship, trust, and the unspoken understanding they share.

This dynamic mirrors how we approach prayer, but it is important to understand that it doesn't mean God is influenced by our praise or that His blessings depend on how eloquently we worship Him. Rather, it reflects the essence of prayer itself – a sacred process that is not driven by desires, but by a deep respect for the divine order. This order, often referred to as Karmkand, is the foundation of Sanatan Dharma, guiding how we perform rituals and offerings. Whether it's the humble act of bowing in a simple Ekopchar (a simple getsure of joining hands in front of the deity) or the grandeur of a Rajasuya Yagya (the grandest yagya where silver, gold, horses, and cows are donated) each form of prayer is a reflection of this sacred order, where devotion and reverence flow from the heart, not the need for reward.

As we explored in Chapter 2, where we delved into God's supreme powers, it's easy to forget something so simple yet so important: God already understands the depths of our desires. After all, He is the creator of the universe, the giver of life, and the source of every emotion we experience. He knows exactly what is best for us, even when we cannot see it. Yet, as human beings, we often fall into the trap of acting in ways that are less than wise - clinging to dissatisfaction, letting our stubbornness lead us, and at times, even behaving like beggars. We ask for things so small, without realizing that in doing so, we may be interrupting the larger, more beautiful plans God has in store for us. Let's take a moment to explore this idea more deeply through an example:

It was just around 11:00 a.m. when Mr. Shah, having wrapped up an early meeting, was on his way home. The morning had been a triumph, and his heart was light with the satisfaction of closing a deal that had been months in the making with one of the city's most esteemed companies. The car hummed smoothly along the road, but as he waited for the traffic light to turn green, his attention was caught by something that pulled at the edges of his contentment. On the sidewalk, a beggar sat slumped, his face drawn and weary, the signs of hunger etched deeply into his features. It was clear that he hadn't eaten in days.

Mr. Shah felt a stirring of empathy. Without hesitation, he pulled his car to a stop and rolled down the window, intending to offer the man a meal. As he approached, the beggar's voice cracked the air, not asking for food, but for something simpler - tea and cookies. The request was humble, yet the need was undeniable. Something in Mr.

Shah's heart softened in that moment. With a quiet nod, he reached into his bag and handed the beggar exactly what he had asked for, considering that's what he needed.

When we pause to think about this situation, who truly had their wish fulfilled, and who walked away with less than they could have? The beggar, despite thinking his desire had been met, was unaware that Mr. Shah had intended to offer him a full meal, something far beyond the simple tea and cookies he asked for. The beggar, with his limited request, settled for less, not knowing that standing there silently might have led to a far greater gift. Much like the beggar, we too often approach life, and God, with small desires - requests that may seem reasonable, yet pale in comparison to what could be ours. If only we trusted in the bigger plans and allowed ourselves to receive the abundance that's waiting, just like Mr. Shah's unspoken generosity.

For me, the question has always been: *Do I really need to ask for anything at all?* As I've grown and learned, I've come to believe that God, the ruler of this vast universe, already knows what I need long before I even realize it myself. How could He not? He sees and understands every corner of my soul, every quiet wish, every unspoken longing. The idea of asking seems almost silly when I trust that He, in His wisdom, has already planned what is best for me at every turn.

This is why I no longer feel the need to ask. Instead, I choose to rest in a deep sense of gratitude for what I've already been given, and I trust that God will continue to provide, in His perfect timing, exactly what I need. The greatest gift, I've learned, is not found in any material possession, but in the quiet, unshakeable assurance that He is always by my side, guiding me, loving me, and walking with me through every moment of my life. As I reflect on this, I realize that true fulfillment doesn't come from chasing desires, but from aligning with the divine flow of life. And so, as we move into the next chapter, we'll explore how to cultivate a heart that not only understands its desires but learns to receive them in the most fulfilling way.

DESIRES

Q4. How do I get my desires fulfilled?

In this world brimming with material pursuits, who among us doesn't carry a heart full of desires? It's human to dream, to yearn for things that bring us happiness, comfort, or a sense of achievement. Some of us chase these dreams with unyielding determination, while others quietly hope for a stroke of luck or a divine hand to grant them with ease.

Whether it's the longing to own luxurious outfits or the ambition to build the house we've envisioned in our daydreams, we often find ourselves wishing for these desires to magically come to life, as if by some unseen force. In the fast-paced era we live in, where answers are only a click away, the concept of manifestation has risen to the forefront - promising a seemingly effortless path to realizing our dreams.

But as enticing as this idea is, it serves as only a fragment of a larger truth. The fulfillment of desires isn't merely about wishful thinking or fleeting trends; it is interwoven with deeper principles that unfold over time, revealing their meaning only when viewed from a broader lens of understanding.

In ancient times, sacrifices, or yagya, were deeply heartfelt expressions of gratitude to the divine for the countless gifts that sustained life. These offerings were not just rituals but acts of devotion, meant to honor the unseen forces that governed the rhythms of existence. People believed that the world thrived in harmony because of these sacrifices, which pleased the deities overseeing nature's delicate balance. (Doniger 1998)

Through yagya, humanity acknowledged the abundance around them - the timely rains that nurtured their crops, the bountiful harvests that filled their granaries, and the shield of protection that kept them safe from misfortune. It was their way of saying thank you for the rocks that provided refuge, the fire that gave warmth and cooked their meals, the water that quenched their thirst and cleansed their bodies, the trees that bore fruit and herbs for healing, and the animals that offered companionship and bore their burdens.

In those days, life was a harmonious symphony, deeply connected to the rhythms of nature. Every breath, every moment, felt intertwined with the world around - a silent understanding that humanity and nature were partners in an eternal dance of give and take. Sacrifices were not mere rituals; they were heartfelt offerings, threads of gratitude woven into the fabric of existence. These acts carried a quiet yet powerful intent - to honor the forces that sustained life, to nurture a balance that brought abundance, safety, and peace. It was a way of saying thank you, a way of keeping the heart of life beating strong and steady.

सहयज्ञाः प्रजाः सृष्ट्वा पुरोवाच प्रजापतिः ।

अनेन प्रसविष्यध्वमेष वोऽस्त्विष्टकामधुक् ॥ 3.10

{In the beginning of creation, God sent forth mankind with sacrifices for Vishnu, blessing them: 'By this sacrifice, may you be happy, for it will bestow upon you everything you need for happiness and liberation.}

देवान् भावयतानेन ते देवा भावयन्तु वः।

परस्परं भावयन्तः श्रेयः परमवाप्स्यथ ॥ 3.11

{The gods, pleased by your sacrifices, will grant you prosperity. And as they are sustained by your offerings, both will thrive through mutual care.}

अन्नाद्भवन्ति भूतानि पर्जन्यादन्नसम्भवः।

यज्ञाद्भवति पर्जन्यो यज्ञः कर्मसमुद्भवः ॥ 3.14

{All creatures depend on food, food grows from rain, and rain is born of sacrifice. Sacrifice, in turn, arises from the performance of prescribed duties.}

Our ancient scriptures vividly describe the divine connection between specific deities and the blessings they bestow. Lord Ganesh, known as the remover of obstacles, is worshipped for a smooth path in life - whether it's overcoming personal challenges, embarking on new ventures, or finding success in marriage. The Ganesh Stotram is recited, and offerings of sweet modaks are made, as gratitude for the fulfilment of wisdom, the removal of personal challenges, and the grace to move forward with confidence; besides Ganesh homa.

Goddess Durga, with her fierce protection and unyielding strength, is invoked courageously to face life's darkest moments, freedom from fear, and empowerment in times of crisis. For instance, someone going through a difficult personal struggle, such as mental health issues, or any emotional crisis, might recite the Durga Saptashati, praying for strength to face these trials with inner power and determination.

Goddess Lakshmi, the embodiment of wealth, abundance, and prosperity, is worshipped for financial stability and material well-being. For those wishing to improve their financial situation, whether it's finding success in business, attracting wealth, or simply creating a comfortable home, Lakshmi's blessings are sought by chanting the Shri Suktam and offering flowers or lighting lamps. Her devotees ask for more than just money - they pray for the kind of abundance that brings peace, joy, and fulfillment.

Furthermore, Shrimad Bhagavata Mahapurana describes which diety to worship for a particular kind of desires. Such as,

श्रीशुक उवाच ।

एवमेतन्निगदितं पृष्टवान्यद्भवान्मम ।
नृणां यन्म्रियमानानां मनुष्येषु मनीषिणाम् ।। 1 ।।

ब्रह्मवर्चसकामस्तु यजेत ब्रह्मणस्पतिम् ।
इन्द्रं इन्द्रियकामस्तु प्रजाकामः प्रजापतीन् ।। 2 ।।

देवीं मायां तु श्रीकामः तेजःकामो विभावसुम् ।
वसुकामो वसून् रुद्रान् वीर्यकामोऽथ वीर्यवान् ।। 3 ।।

अन्नाद्यकामस्त्वदितिं स्वर्गकामोऽदितेः सुतान् ।
विश्वान्देवान्राज्यकामः साध्यान्संसाधको विशाम् ।। 4 ।।

आयुष्कामोऽश्विनौ देवौ पुष्टिकाम इळां यजेत् ।
प्रतिष्ठाकामः पुरुषो रोदसी लोकमातरौ ।। 5 ।।

रूपाभिकामो गन्धर्वान् स्त्रीकामोऽप्सर उर्वशीम् ।
आधिपत्यकामः सर्वेषां यजेत परमेष्ठिनम् ।। 6 ।।

यज्ञं यजेत यशःकामः कोशकामः प्रचेतसम् ।
विद्याकामस्तु गिरिशं दाम्पत्यार्थ उमा सतीम् ।। 7 ।।

धर्मार्थ उत्तमश्लोकं तन्तुं तन्वन् पितृन् यजेत् ।
रक्षा कामः पुण्यजनान् ओजःकामो मरुद्गणान् ।। 8 ।।

राज्यकामो मनून् देवान् निरृतिं त्वभिचरन् यजेत् ।
कामकामो यजेत्सोमं अकामः पुरुषं परम् ।। 9 ।।

अकामः सर्वकामो वा मोक्षकाम उदारधीः ।
तीव्रेण भक्तियोगेन यजेत पुरुषं परम् ।। 10 ।।

{Shri Sukadev said: For the intelligent among men, I have given you all the answers in response to the inquiring of your good self about the human being on the threshold of death. They who desire the luster of the Absolute worship the master of the Vedas [Brihaspati], Indra, the king of heaven is there for the ones desiring the strength of the senses [sex] and the Prajâpatis [the strong progenitors] are there for those who desire offspring. The goddess [Durgâ] is there for those who desire the beauty of the material world, the fire god is there for the ones desiring power, for wealth there are the Vasus [a type of demigod] and the incarnations of Rudra [Lord S'iva] are there for those who wish strength and heroism. For a good harvest the mother of the demigods Aditi is worshiped, desiring heaven one worships her sons, for those desiring royal riches there are the Vishwadev demigods and to be of commercial success there are the Sadhya gods. The As'vinîs [two demigod brothers] are there for the ones desiring longevity, for a strong body mother earth is worshiped and those who want to maintain their position and be renown respect the goddesses of the earth and the heavens. Aspiring beauty there are the heavenly Gandharva, those who want a good wife seek the girls of the heavenly society [the Apsaras and Urvas'îs] and anyone who wants to dominate others is bound to the worship of Brahmâ, the head of the universe. Yajña, the Lord of Sacrifice is worshiped for tangible fame and for a good bank balance Varuna, the treasurer, is sought. But those who desire to learn, worship S'iva himself while for a good marriage his chaste wife Umâ is honored.

For spiritual progress the supreme truth [Lord Vishnu and His devotees] is worshiped, for offspring and their care one seeks the ancestral [the residents of Pitriloka], pious persons are sought by those who seek protection, while the demigods in general are there for standing strong in life. The godly Manus [the fathers of mankind] are there for those desiring a kingdom, but the demons are sought for defeating enemies. The ones desiring sense gratification are bound to the moon [Chandra], while those who are free from desire worship the Supreme Personality in the beyond.}

Even when we seek guidance from astrologers for the fulfillment of our desires, they often recommend simple yet meaningful offerings. These might include offering water to a Shivling, the Sun, or sacred trees like the Banyan or Pipal tree, Tulsi plant or flowing rivers. We are also encouraged to feed cows, dogs, or other animals as a way of giving back to the world. While a yagya, which is time-consuming and involves multiple ingredients, is considered a powerful offering, even in its simplest form, the act of offering something - whether it's water, food, or care - plays a vital role in opening the path to fulfillment - we are having a sense of offering these (yagya ingredients) to God. How powerful would that be in contrast to that of the former mentioned offerings! This exchange of energy, no matter how small, is believed to create space for new energy to flow.

Picture a gardener who spends hours tending to plants, carefully nurturing them with water, sunlight, and love. Over time, the garden flourishes, bursting with vibrant flowers and lush greenery. The gardener doesn't expect anything in return but continues to care for the plants, watching them grow. One day, a passerby notices the beauty of the garden and pauses to admire it. They may take a moment to appreciate the beauty, but how often do they stop to thank the gardener for the time and effort that went into making it so? Just as we often overlook the gardener's hard work, many times we fail to recognize the unseen hands that provide us with life's blessings. Whether it's the sun that warms our skin, the food that nourishes us, or the love that surrounds us, all of it comes from a source beyond our control, deserving of gratitude, not just simple enjoyment.

इष्टान्भोगान्हि वो देवा दास्यन्ते यज्ञभाविता: ।

तेर्दत्तानप्रदायेभ्यो यो भुङ्क्ते स्तेन एव सः ॥ 3.12

{One who consumes the gifts of the gods without offering back is nothing but a thief.}

Even the most powerful kings, such as Dashratha, engaged in yagyas, not merely to fulfill personal desires, but to inspire others toward a life of virtue and righteousness.

These sacred rituals were performed with deep intentions - to bless the land with rain, to ensure success in battle, to heal from illnesses, or even to ask for the blessing of children through ceremonies like the Putrakameshti yagya (Rao 2024). Each sacrifice held a meaningful purpose, rooted in the belief that these acts could bring about positive change, both personally and for the greater good.

The Vedas guide us not only in performing these rituals, but also in understanding the deeper essence of the materials involved. Ingredients like ghee and herbs are not just offerings; they have a transformative power, purifying the environment and the soul alike (S, A, and V 2018). They symbolize the cleansing of both body and spirit, and their use in the yagyas serves to elevate the atmosphere, allowing one to draw closer to the divine. This sacred process, more than a mere ritual, is a way to connect with the higher forces and invoke blessings for the well-being of all.

कर्मणैव हि संसिद्धिमास्थिता जनकादयः ।

लोकसङ्ग्रहमेवापि सम्पश्यन्कर्तुमर्हसि ॥ 3.20

{Kings such as Janka attained perfection solely by performance of prescribed duties. Therefore, just for the sake of educating the people in general, you should perform your action.}

कर्म ब्रह्मोद्भवं विद्धि ब्रह्माक्षरसमुद्भवम्।

तस्मात्सर्वगतं ब्रह्म नित्यं यज्ञे प्रतिष्ठितम् ॥ 3.15

{Regulated duties are rooted in the Vedas, which are the manifestation of the divine. Therefore, the divine is ever-present in acts of sacrifice.}

एवं प्रवर्तितं चक्रं नानुवर्तयतीह यः।

अघायुरिन्द्रियारामो मोघं पार्थ स जीवति॥ 3.16

{One who does not follow this cycle of sacrifice, living only for personal pleasure, leads a sinful life. Such a person lives in vain.}

Some might argue that modern society doesn't need to follow these ancient practices. They might view rituals as outdated, unnecessary, or even a waste of time. But is this dismissive attitude truly based on understanding? These traditions are not merely old customs - they are deeply rooted into balance, guiding us in how to give and receive, act and accept the consequences. While Western progress has brought many valuable advancements, turning our backs on the wisdom of our roots risks losing something irreplaceable. Progress is important, but it's equally crucial to stay connected to the traditions that have shaped us, grounding ourselves in what truly nurtures our souls.

यज्ञशिष्टामृतभुजो यान्ति ब्रह्म सनातनम्।

नायं लोकोऽस्त्ययज्ञस्य कुतोऽन्यः कुरुसत्तम ॥ 4.39

{Without sacrifice, happiness is unattainable on this earth or in the life beyond. What hope is there for joy elsewhere?}

Sacrifice is more than just following rituals; it's a heartfelt gesture of gratitude. It's a reminder that the blessings we have are not solely the result of our own efforts. Whether or not you believe in a higher power, the act of being thankful brings a sense of balance to life. In many ways, even the modern idea of manifestation is rooted in this truth. When we take a moment to appreciate what we already have, we open ourselves to more of life's gifts. True fulfillment isn't found in hoarding or taking more, but in the act of giving - it’s through rituals, meaningful actions, or simply offering a sincere thank-you. It’s in those moments of giving that we find a deeper connection to what truly matters.

Without sacrifice, whether it’s something we can touch or something that comes from deep within, life begins to feel empty. It’s through letting go and giving something of ourselves that we open up room for the blessings that are waiting to enter. It’s the exchange that keeps the cycle of life full, allowing us to find meaning and connection in everything we do. Each time we give, we invite new energy and possibilities to fill our hearts and our lives. Just as we breathe in and out, giving is essential to receiving.

HEALING

Q5. Is it possible for people to heal themselves in this materially inclined world?

As children, our lives are shaped not just by the company we keep but also by the environment we grow up in. Parents often keep a close watch on the friends we make, the people who influence us, and how we spend our time. Yet, how often do they stop to look inward and ask themselves: Is our home a safe haven for our child's emotions? Does it offer the warmth, understanding, and love needed to nurture a healthy mind? And even more importantly, are we, as parents, in a place of emotional stability to guide and support this young soul?

A child's world begins at home - it is their sanctuary, their second womb, offering comfort and protection long after birth. The walls of this space hold the power to shape their thoughts, feelings, character, and sense of self. A mother, often the child's first teacher, is not just the giver of life but also the one who imparts the earliest lessons of love, compassion, and resilience. Her words, her actions, and even her silences leave imprints on the child's heart, forming the foundation of their emotional world.

The home is more than a roof over a child's head; it is the first school of life, the place where they learn how to love, trust, and dream. A child absorbs not just what is said but also what is felt - unspoken tensions, silent affections, or unresolved struggles. The atmosphere parents create within their home becomes the soil where their child's mind grows. Will it bloom with confidence and joy, or will it struggle under the weight of unspoken burdens? These are the questions we must dare to ask ourselves if we truly want to raise emotionally healthy and happy individuals.

But what happens when parents are drained emotionally, their reserves of patience and love running thin? How can they pour their love into their child's heart when their own feels empty? A parent struggling to make ends meet might find even the simplest, most innocent questions from their child overwhelming, sparking frustration that sometimes erupts into harsh words or unintended anger. These moments can leave lasting marks on the child, creating confusion and a sense of rejection.

When a parent is burdened with mental unrest, their ability to respond to their child's emotional needs can waver. A child's small victories might go unnoticed, their fears unheard, leaving them to feel invisible and alone. This lack of connection can push them toward external sources of comfort, which may not always have their best interests at heart.

I have seen time and again that any deficiency in a

parent's life - be it physical exhaustion, financial struggles, or emotional instability - inevitably leaves an imprint on the child's mind. It seeps into their world, influencing how they perceive themselves and their place in the family. When parents lose their temper or are too preoccupied with their own battles, the moments that should be filled with love, laughter, and reassurance slip away. The precious gift of quality time, which could strengthen the parent-child bond, becomes a rarity. And in its absence, the child grows up feeling disconnected, often carrying those scars into adulthood.

Crossroads of Regret

Let me take you back in the 70's to the life of a vibrant young woman, Nirmala - a 19-year-old with dreams as big as her heart. She was a rare combination of talent, ambition, and grace, someone who could light up any room with her presence. Her love for music was unmatched; she sang on a weekly TV show, her voice carrying the kind of emotion that touched hearts. Cooking was another passion, a way she expressed love and creativity, while her prowess on the baseball field, where she played at the national level, revealed her fierce determination and spirit.

Though her family didn't have much in terms of material wealth, they were rich in values and warmth. The youngest of four sisters and two brothers, she grew up in a bustling household filled with chatter, laughter, and shared struggles. Her parents doted on her endlessly, seeing her as the sparkling gem of their family. Despite their modest means, they nurtured her dreams, giving her the strength and confidence to chase them. This was a time when life was simple but full of love, and an unshakable belief that with courage and effort, dreams could be turned into reality.

It was during the preparations for her third sister's wedding, a time filled with joy, chaos, and family togetherness. As was tradition, each sibling was given a special gift - a piece of jewelry or a beautiful outfit, thoughtfully chosen as a token of love and appreciation. Amid the excitement, her heart longed for something simple yet meaningful - a thread-like, delicate silver chain. She had imagined how it would feel around her neck, a small treasure she could call her own.

But when she timidly voiced her desire, her parents, with kind yet weary expressions, explained that their resources were stretched thin thinking that being the smartest and most compassionate among their children, she would understand the crisis. They reassured her of their love, but their words couldn't soothe the ache in her heart. She watched as her siblings gleefully unwrapped their gifts, their laughter filling the room, while her own wish remained unfulfilled. It wasn't about the chain itself - it was the feeling of being seen, of having her smallest yearning understood and honored.

That day, she stayed by her parent's side as they bustled through markets, checking off endless wedding lists. She smiled when spoken to and helped wherever needed, but her appetite for the celebratory treats, for the joy of the occasion, had vanished. Every shop they visited reminded her of the little silver chain she could not have.

When night fell, the weight of her emotions became too heavy to bear. Alone in her room, she let the tears flow, her heart heavy with a mix of love and longing. She wasn't upset with her parents - they had always done their best - but she couldn't shake the sadness of being overlooked in a moment that mattered to her. The unfulfilled wish wasn't just about the chain; it felt like a reflection of her place in the family - her own little world, a tender reminder of how even the smallest disappointments can leave invisible scars on a young, vulnerable heart. That night, as she cried herself to sleep, she promised herself she would never let someone else feel the way she did - unseen, unheard, and unacknowledged.

This seemingly insignificant incident left a lasting mark on her heart, embedding a sense of emotional unease that she couldn't quite shake. On the surface, life appeared to carry on as usual - the gentle rhythm of her early morning walks, the hum of activity at college, and the moments she poured her soul into singing at the television studio. But beneath her bright and composed exterior, a quiet ache had taken root. It wasn't loud or demanding, but it was there, settling into the corners of her being. The world saw her smile, heard the melody in her voice, and marveled at her grace, yet she carried within her a wound that no one seemed to notice. The hurt lingered, unspoken and unseen, like a shadow cast on a sunny day - subtle, yet impossible to ignore.

One afternoon, as she walked home lost in her thoughts, she crossed paths with a boy whose eyes had followed her for some time. He had been drawn to her quiet allure - her graceful sense of style, the subtle glow of her skin, and the unspoken confidence she carried. He had often seen her around campus, catching glimpses of her in fleeting moments, each one deepening his admiration for her.

This time, he finally mustered the courage to approach her. He stood tall with a dusky complexion, his bold demeanor complemented by an easy smile. A football player with an artistic soul, Dhirendra, carried an air of spontaneity that made him impossible to ignore. His personality was vibrant, unapologetically outspoken, and his humor seemed to fill every corner of a room.

When he invited her to meet him, she hesitated briefly but accepted. There was something about his openness that disarmed her, something that felt like a gentle pull away from the solitude she had grown too accustomed to. Her heart, burdened by the weight of loneliness, longed for an anchor, and his offer felt like a small but significant escape. For the first time in a while, she allowed herself to consider the possibility of companionship, a fragile hope stirring quietly within her.

Within just a few days of knowing each other, he casually brought up the idea of marriage, almost as if it were an afterthought. To her own surprise, and perhaps even to his, she said yes. What they didn't understand at that moment was the deeper undercurrent driving their decisions. For him, the proposal wasn't an act of love or commitment; it was his ego speaking, a way to claim her and prove something to himself for his complexion and the remarks he often heard about it. For her, the acceptance wasn't rooted in joy or clarity; it came from a place of pain, a response shaped by the wounds she had yet to heal. superficially, both had their own reasons to accompany each other but that would last a little.

They entered into marriage with haste, swept up in the illusion that it could fill the empty spaces within them. Neither paused to question their true intentions or whether they were ready to build a life together. The ceremony became a blur of promises made without understanding the weight of their meaning. In their rush to find what they thought they were missing, they overlooked the truth - that love born of ego and pain often carries a heavy price.

Their impulsive decision set off a storm that shook both families to their core. Her father and brother were livid, their anger burning bright with betrayal, while the boy's family cast their disapproval like a shadow over their choice. In the aftermath, they were forced to distance themselves from the people they loved most. For a brief moment, in their new world, the couple found peace in each other. They spent evenings under the stars, driving aimlessly through the night, their hearts light with laughter and the promise of a future together. Their spontaneous trips felt like a sweet escape, a dream where they were the only two souls that mattered.

But it wasn't long before cracks began to appear. The man she once admired began to reveal a side of himself she never could have imagined. The warmth of their early days faded, replaced by a chilling pattern of late nights filled with alcohol, and moments when the man, once gentle, became an unrecognizable monster. His anger, once held back, spilled over. He started coming home drunk, his words harsh and cutting, his hands no longer tender but violent - maybe from the external influence of the company he had kept or his certain underlying self. She conceived in the first year of their marriage. Even in a time when she needed love and care the most, he continued to hurt her, beat her while being drunk and kick her in the belly. The pain was not just physical, but emotional, as she endured the unbearable cruelty, hoping for a change that never came. The love she once believed in was now twisted into something dark and unforgiving.

Caught in a relentless cycle of love and violence, she stayed in the marriage, weighed down more by the fear of society's judgment than by her own pain. Once a bright, independent young woman with dreams and hope in her heart, her world had now shrunk to one of survival. The days blurred together as she endured the abuse, not only for her own sake but also to shield her unborn child from the harsh reality of a broken family. She clung to the idea of protecting her child from the shame that might come with a disrupted home, even as it tore at her soul. Each day, she sacrificed her own happiness and peace, holding onto the belief that staying in this marriage would somehow keep her child safe from the weight of judgment that would fall upon them.

Despite the unbearable pain she carried, she poured every ounce of her love into raising her son, Umang. She vowed that her struggles would never spill over into his life. No matter how cruel his father was, she wrapped Umang in the tender embrace of a mother's love, shielding him as best as she could. In the dead of night, when the weight of her frustrations felt like it might crush her, she bit her trembling lip, wiped her tears, and knelt before her God. Prayer became her refuge, her solace - a quiet plea for strength to endure another day.

But no prayer could silence the chaos that raged within their home. His father, lost to drunk fury, unleashed his anger on both of them. Umang bore more than his small shoulders should have ever carried. A slap here, a harsh word there, sometimes worse. He learned to flinch at the smallest of movements, the faintest changes in tone. The distant rumble of his father's scooter on the road became his signal to run - to hide. Panic would seize his tiny heart as he scrambled to find a spot, anywhere, to escape. More often than not, it was the cramped corner near the bookshelf where he would squeeze himself in, burying his face in old books, as though the musty pages could swallow him whole, away from the nightmare that was his reality.

And yet, she never let his light dim. Every evening, she sat by his side, telling him stories of gods and warriors, of battles fought not just with swords but with courage and integrity, hoping that one day he would become a man with a heart full of compassion, far different from the one who had brought him into the world.

She filled his nights with dreams of kindness, of compassion, of a world better than the one he knew. She bore her wounds silently, her heart breaking anew every time she saw the fear in his eyes. But even in that fear, she found a reason to keep going. Umang was her hope, her reason to endure her hard life.

Years went by, but the longing for the love she had never known still lingered deep within her heart, like a silent void that refused to fade. It was always there, quietly pulling at her, reminding her of what was missing. Though throughout twenty-two years of marriage, she kept herself busy with earning a little from her life skills, which she would mostly spend on her heart - her son. Then, one day, on her way home on a bus, she met someone. A man who gave her the warmth, affection, and respect she had always dreamed of. In their first conversation, that man told her that she looked lost and empty, as if she needed a shoulder to rest her head on. She replied saying she was tortured the night before. This torture had continued for 22 years and nothing of it had changed in all this while.

But for the first time in what felt like forever, she felt seen and valued. In his presence, the love that had been dormant inside her began to bloom once more. It was as if the world had shifted, and she was finally alive again, ready to leave behind the years of quiet suffering and emotional emptiness. But in that moment of overwhelming emotion, when everything seemed to promise a new beginning, she found herself torn. The thought crossed her mind - could she walk away from everything, including her son, to follow this newfound passion, to embrace a love that seemed so right in that moment? It was a fleeting, desperate thought born from the intensity of her emotions, but it left her heart heavy with conflict.

However, fate had other plans. In a few months, her son stumbled upon the secret affair that had been hidden for so long. He was seventeen when this discovery tore at his heart, but instead of anger, he approached her with compassion, trying to see things through her eyes, hoping to understand the pain she had carried as a woman. Although, what he encountered was an emotional wall - his mother's indifference to his own hurt left him speechless. It was then that he truly saw the depth of the wounds she had never healed. For the first time, he understood how her past, filled with unresolved pain, had shaped every decision she made, pushing her to act in ways that now seemed cold and distant. The realization hit him like a sharp blow - this invisible trauma had quietly built a wall between them, breaking the closeness they once shared and leaving him grappling with a new, painful understanding of his mother.

It felt like the world had turned upside down. The woman who had been his sanctuary, his protector, the one who shielded him from his father's rage and loved him with a tenderness he thought unbreakable, was now ready to leave him behind. For someone else. A stranger was worth more to her now than her own child and the bond they had built through years of struggle and love. The thought alone was unbearable, like a knife twisting in his chest.

He couldn't understand it. The very thought of it felt like betrayal wrapped in disbelief. His mother, the one person he trusted blindly, the only source of love and safety in his chaotic world, was choosing someone else over him. How could she? Didn't she see how much he needed her, how much he loved her? How could the woman who had once cherished him above all, who had been his refuge from his father's rage, now abandon him for a stranger?

Every moment they'd shared, every promise she'd silently made through her gentle touch, now felt like a cruel lie. If she, the one person who had always been there, could leave so easily, what was the point of trusting anyone else in this world? The world around him felt unstable, like the ground beneath his feet had crumbled, leaving him suspended in a void.

The pain was suffocating, raw and relentless, and he didn't know how to escape it. He withdrew, piece by piece, from everyone and everything. He stopped meeting his friends, stopped laughing at jokes, stopped caring about the things that once brought him joy. Instead, he retreated into the confines of his own mind, where it felt safer, quieter.

But even there, the emptiness followed him like a shadow - a hollow ache that refused to leave.

At night, he lay awake, staring at the ceiling, his chest tight with questions that had no answers. Did he not deserve her love anymore? Tears would silently roll down his cheeks as he remembered the woman who once cradled him in her arms, whispering that she would always be there. Now, even that memory felt tainted, leaving him with nothing but the cold realization that the love he thought was unshakable had been nothing more than an illusion. Though she didn't leave the family physically, her actions made her distant from her son while still living under the same roof.

This story tells us to reflect on some deep, emotional questions: Could the son have accepted his mother's choices if he had not carried the burden of emotional scars? Could the mother's pain have been kept from affecting her child if she had taken the time to heal on her own? These questions tug at the heart, reminding us of how the unresolved hurts we carry can shape the lives of those closest to us, often in ways we never intended. It's a powerful reminder of how healing, both for ourselves and for those we love, is not just a gift, but a responsibility.

A mother is often called a child's first teacher, the one who shapes their early world with care, love, and lessons of right and wrong. She may have poured her heart into raising her son, guiding him with the best of intentions, trying to fill his life with warmth and wisdom. Yet, even with all her love, she might have unknowingly failed to nurture him emotionally. But can she truly be blamed for this? After all, the weight of her own struggles - her pain, her past - was something she carried, and perhaps, it became too much to bear. She too was a victim of life's harsh realities.

The son, in turn, grew up surrounded by the harshness of his father's toxic behavior. He saw the drinking, the violence, the chaos that tore apart their home, leaving deep scars on his young heart. He witnessed cruelty, not only in the form of physical abuse but in the silent wounds of neglect and fear that filled their home. These moments of dark experiences, became part of who he was, deeply imprinted in his soul. He couldn't escape the weight of that pain, and so, the cycle continued.

In this way, both the mother and son were bound by their own struggles - each trying to do their best, but both scarred by the shadows of their past. How can we fully understand the depth of someone's actions without considering the life they've lived, the burdens they've carried, and the love they've tried to give despite it all?

Healing was a necessity she could no longer ignore. If she had taken the time to heal from the wounds of her childhood - if she hadn't placed her happiness in the hands of things like a piece of jewelry or searched for love in places outside herself or her family - maybe things would have turned out differently. If only she had learned to see the world through her son's innocent eyes, perhaps her actions would have been driven more by love and care instead of a deep, unfulfilled longing. Healing isn't just about mending what's broken within; it's about breaking the chain of pain that could otherwise be passed on. Without it, trauma becomes something we unintentionally leave behind, affecting those we care about most.

As the years of her life began to wind down, guilt wrapped itself around the mother's heart, pulling her deeper into regret. She couldn't escape the weight of her past, especially the affair that had torn her family apart and made her feel like she had committed a sin. It haunted her thoughts, each memory a sharp reminder of choices that had left wounds, both in herself and in those she loved. But over time, as the days blurred into years, she found herself seeking something more - something that could bring her peace.

She was fifty-three when, in her search for comfort, she turned to the Bhagavad Geeta, a book that promised answers to life's most painful questions. Each day, she sat quietly with its pages, allowing the wisdom within them to slowly wash over her. She wasn't looking for easy forgiveness but for a way to understand her actions, to come to terms with the mistakes she had made. She read the verses, hoping that through their guidance, she could release herself from the grip of guilt that had bound her for so long. Slowly, with each passing day, the weight on her heart began to feel lighter, as if the words she read were gently cleansing her, one page at a time.

अपि चेदसि पापेभ्य: सर्वेभ्य: पापकृत्तम: ।
सर्वं ज्ञानप्लवेनेव वृजिनं सन्तरिष्यसि ॥ 4.36

{Even if you are considered the most sinful of all sinners, when you are situated in the boat of transcendental knowledge, you will cross over the ocean of miseries.}

Through quiet moments of prayer, deep reflection, and the steady rhythm of chanting mantras each day, she slowly began to let go of the weight she had been carrying. With each prayer, she felt the walls around her heart soften, as if the very act of devotion was cleansing her soul. She gave herself the gift of forgiveness, not all at once, but bit by bit, each moment of surrender a small step toward healing. As she immersed herself more in her spiritual practice, a sense of calm washed over her - one she had long yearned for but couldn't find in the busyness of life. The Bhagavad Geeta gently reminded her that no matter how heavy the mistakes of the past, redemption was always within reach for those who sought it with an open heart and a genuine desire to change. In this sacred space of devotion, she found the peace she had been searching for, and in that peace, she rediscovered herself.

अपि चेत्सुदुराचारो भजते मामनन्यभाक् ।

साधुरेव स मन्तव्य: सम्यग्व्यवसितो हि सः ॥ 9.30

{Even if one commits the most abominable actions, if they are devoted to Me, they are to be considered saintly because they are properly situated in their determination.}

This story reminds us that even the smallest actions we take can have a lasting impact, not just on others, but also on ourselves. In today's world, many young girls often feel upset when their parents place restrictions on them - whether it's about what they wear or where they can go with their friends. These rules can stir up deep feelings of frustration, making them feel misunderstood or even resentful. It's easy for these young hearts to become overwhelmed with emotion, unable to see beyond the moment and understand the deeper care behind the restrictions. They may struggle to comprehend that their parents' decisions are grounded in love and concern for their safety, not an attempt to control their freedom.

In such moments, it's important for parents to approach the situation with both empathy and wisdom. They must recognize the emotional turbulence their children experience and try to connect with their feelings, while also making decisions that are in their best interest. By showing sensitivity to their child's emotional state, and by speaking with care, parents can help build trust and understanding. It's not just about setting rules - it's about creating an environment where children feel heard, supported, and protected. By balancing emotional awareness with practical decision-making, parents can nurture their child's mental well-being and strengthen the bond of trust, even when difficult decisions are made.

Unresolved traumas have a way of seeping through the generations, often without us realizing it. Our emotional wounds, when left unhealed, don't just affect us - they can find their way into the lives of those we love, subtly shaping their experiences. Healing ourselves isn't just about our own peace; it's about breaking the cycle and preventing the weight of our pain from being passed down. Just as Nirmala found solace and healing through spirituality, we too can discover a way to move forward. Healing doesn't mean forgetting the past, but learning from it, letting go of its hold, and choosing to walk a different path. It's a journey towards wholeness - finding the love and peace within ourselves first, so we can share it freely and without burden. Only then can we truly give love to others, untainted by the shadows of our unmet needs.

In the Bhagavad Geeta, Krishna has promised us that if we surrender ourselves to him with trust and devotion, he will shield us from the consequences of our actions. What more reassurance could we possibly need? His love is not just a comfort; it's a source of strength. He has the power to heal the deepest wounds within us, and not just that - he can help rebuild us from the inside out. In his embrace, we find the courage to rise above our past mistakes, to forgive ourselves, and to move forward with a renewed sense of purpose. His protection is a promise, not just for the body, but for the heart and soul as well. With him, we are never truly broken; we are always being mended and made whole again.

REVENGE

Q6. Shall we forgive or seek revenge when someone betrays us?

When betrayal strikes, it cuts deep, leaving an ache that words can barely touch. It feels as if the ground beneath our feet has crumbled, pulling us into a void of confusion and pain. The haunting question "Why me?" echoes endlessly, offering no peace. The heart wrestles with disbelief: "I gave everything I had, trusted with all my being - how could they do this to me?"

Even in the company of those who care, an overwhelming sense of isolation wraps around us, and loneliness becomes an unwelcome companion. The silence of the night amplifies the storm within as thoughts spiral out of control. Memories replay like a relentless loop, and the desire to undo the pain gnaws at our spirit. Anxiety creeps into the quiet moments, turning them into a battleground of emotions. The longing for things to go back to how they were feels almost unbearable.

In this turmoil, the temptation to seek revenge flares up - a desperate attempt to tip the scales of justice. But amid the anger and hurt, a question whispers softly yet powerfully: "Who am I to seek revenge?"

Is revenge truly the answer? Will it give us what we originally wanted? Perhaps the answer lies in silence, in the space where anger cools and reason speaks. Too often, we tread paths fraught with peril, convinced that striking back will mend what was broken within us. Yet, instead of quenching the fire, revenge often fans the flames, leaving scars far deeper than the ones we set out to avenge.

In our quest to even the scales, we risk losing sight of who we are. The desire for vengeance can consume us, turning our pain into a relentless storm. What begins as an attempt to soothe our hearts often ends with us drowning in regret. The true cost of revenge isn't measured in what we do to others but in what it takes from us.

The Weight of Letting Go

Bhavya, at 23, found herself utterly captivated by Kush, a man who was already committed to someone else. Her heart ached, but her hope burned brighter. With an unwavering belief that destiny would one day unite them, she chose to wait - not for days or months, but for seven long years.

Those years carried their share of silent heartbreak. Bhavya stood by Kush as a steadfast friend, silently shouldering the weight of her unspoken love. She laughed with him, listened to his worries, and celebrated his joys, all while her own heart quietly longed for more. Each shared moment was a delicate balance between companionship and yearning.

As the seasons changed and years passed, Kush's relationship came to an end. It was after few months of his break up, that Bhavya gathered all her courage and finally opened her heart to him. Her love, nurtured by years of patience and silent devotion, found its voice. What followed was the beginning of a relationship deeply rooted in their strong friendship - a love story shaped by trust, understanding, and the enduring strength of Bhavya's waiting heart.

Their love story had all the makings of a fairy tale. After

a year of being inseparable, Kush and Bhavya decided to take the next big step and get married. Kush had always dreamt of building a life in Australia, and soon after their wedding, that dream turned into reality. He flew to the land of new beginnings, assuring Bhavya that their reunion was only a matter of time, tied to the completion of her immigration process.

But life had other plans. The paperwork stretched longer than expected, keeping Bhavya tied to India. While her in-laws treated her with the warmth and daughter-like care, she chose to stay with her own parents. It wasn't a rejection of their love but rather a quiet yearning to be in the comfort of the home she had grown up in, waiting for the day she would join Kush across oceans.

Kush stood by her dreams, helping her start her small business and providing the financial support she needed, even though he knew she wouldn't run it for long. She was bound to join him overseas soon, and he wanted to make sure she had everything she desired. From a distance, he remained her rock - always there for her emotionally and financially, offering a steady presence even when miles apart. Yet, as the months went by, a change began to take root within Bhavya. She started pulling away, not only from Kush's family but, more heart-wrenchingly, from Kush himself. The connection that once felt so strong began to fade, and she found herself drifting into a quiet solitude that left him questioning what had shifted between them.

When Kush came back to India, filled with hope and the longing to rekindle the connection they once shared, he was crushed to find out that Bhavya had already found someone else in the brief six months they had been apart. His heart, shattered yet still deeply in love, ached as he desperately asked her to reconsider their marriage. He promised to change, to become whatever she needed, though he knew deep down he had always tried his best. But Bhavya, with a quiet strength in her eyes, stood firm. Her heart had shifted, and there was no going back.

The betrayal shattered Kush, as if the very foundation of his soul had been ripped apart. Grief settled heavily within him, an aching emptiness that no words could fill, and yet, his sorrow remained unspoken. His family, desperate to see him take action, urged him to fight back, to confront Bhavya's family and reveal the truth. They wanted him to reclaim his dignity, to make her face the consequences of her actions. But Kush, deeply anchored in the wisdom of Krishn, chose a path few could understand.

Instead of retaliating, instead of letting his pain dictate his actions, he chose to embrace the situation with quiet acceptance, knowing that this was somehow part of a bigger, divine plan. His heart ached, but he did not allow it to consume him with bitterness. Though the truth could have been weaponized - he could have exposed Bhavya's secrets, dismantling her carefully constructed world, and forced her to confront what she had done - he refused. Not out of weakness, but out of a deep, quiet respect for the love he had once shared with her. What they had was sacred, and even in the face of betrayal, he honored that sacredness by not turning it into something ugly.

There were times when rage consumed Kush, making his chest tighten with fury. He could have easily struck back, exposed Bhavya's deceit, or made her feel the weight of her choices. But each time, a question whispered in his mind, "Will this really bring me peace?" As someone who cherished his devotion to Krishn, Kush found comfort in knowing that not everything in life was meant to be understood or controlled by human hands. He chose to let Bhavya go, realizing that true strength doesn't lie in holding on to resentment, but in setting free those we once loved - even when their actions break us. In that release, he found the quiet courage of letting go.

In Kush's perception, the idea of seeking revenge felt like a never-ending loop, one that would only deepen the wounds of his soul. He realized that no matter how much anger he fed into the fire, it wouldn't erase the hurt, nor would it bring back the trust that had been shattered. It wouldn't heal the scars left by the betrayal, nor would it offer him the peace he so desperately sought. Instead of holding onto the bitterness, he turned to meditation and devotion to Krishn, allowing himself to find solace in the quiet stillness of his heart. Choosing peace over mess, he understood something deeply: letting go, though difficult and often painful, was the key to breaking free. It was the most freeing thing he could do for himself, even if it meant releasing what had once held him captive. His choice to embrace peace, instead of the chaos that revenge promised, became his silent but powerful act of liberation.

*

The ancient epic *Mahabharata* delves deeply into the complex emotions surrounding revenge. In the heart of the battlefield at Kurukshetra, Arjun found himself torn between his duty and his love for his family. As the sounds of war echoed around him, he was confronted with an impossible choice: to fight against his own kin in the name of justice. In the midst of this turmoil, when his heart was heavy with sorrow and confusion, he spoke these words:

न हि प्रपश्यामि ममापनुद्याद् यच्छोकमुच्छोषणमिन्द्रियाणाम्।
अवाप्य भूमावसपत्नमृद्धं राज्यं सुराणामपि चाधिपत्यम्॥ 2.8॥

{I can find no means to drive away this grief which is drying up my senses. I will not be able to dispel it, even if I win a prosperous, unrivaled kingdom on earth with sovereignty like the demigods in heaven.}

Like Kush, Arjun found himself caught in the same emotional struggle - orn between the decision to stand firm or let go. In the beginning, he was overwhelmed by a deep sorrow that held him in place, unsure of what to do. His heart ached, not wanting to hurt those he loved, even though they had caused him pain. The weight of this inner turmoil made every choice feel unbearable. But Krishn, in his wisdom, spoke to him, reminding Arjun that attachment clouds our judgment. He showed him that true strength lies not in fighting every battle, but in recognizing which ones are truly worth standing up for. In that moment, Arjun realized that wisdom is not always about being right or proving a point - it's about knowing when to act with love and when to let go with grace.

There is a thin line between standing up for oneself and seeking revenge to satisfy ego. When we are wronged, it's natural to feel the need to defend our dignity. Standing up for ourselves in those moments is not just about setting boundaries - it's a reminder that we value our own self-respect. It's a way of reclaiming our power, of asserting that we deserve to be treated with fairness and kindness. However, revenge, fueled by anger and a desire to make others feel the pain they caused, often leaves us feeling more hollow than satisfied. It doesn't heal the wounds or restore peace. As Krishn teaches in the Geeta, true strength lies not in seeking vengeance, but in letting go of resentment and choosing a path of peace. In doing so, we find a sense of inner calm that no external action can provide.

अशोच्यानन्वशोचस्त्वं प्रज्ञावादांश्च भाषसे ।

गतासूनगतासूंश्च नानुशोचन्ति पण्डिताः ॥ 2.99 ॥

{The supreme personality of Godhead said: While speaking learned words you are mourning for what is not worthy of grief. Those who are wise lament neither for the living nor for the dead.}

मात्रास्पर्शास्तु कोन्तेय शीतोष्णसुखदुःखदाः ।

आगमापायिनोऽनित्यास्तांस्तितिक्षस्व भारत ॥ 2.94 ॥

{O Son of Kunti, the non permanent appearance of happiness and distress, their disappearance in due course are like the disappearance and appearance of winter and summer seasons. They arise from sense perception, O Scion of Bharata, and one must learn to tolerate them without being disturbed.}

Seeking revenge is like holding onto a burning rope, unwilling to let go, even though it only causes more pain. In trying to hurt those who hurt us, we only bind ourselves to their actions, letting our suffering linger far longer than necessary. True freedom, however, comes from the ability to step away – not from apathy, but from the understanding that some things are beyond our control, and that holding on only traps us in the past. Letting go isn't forgetting; it's giving ourselves the peace to heal, unburdened by the weight of resentment.

Kush's story serves as a powerful reminder that while betrayal can wound us in ways that seem impossible to heal, it is our response that shapes the person we become. Forgiveness is not a sign of weakness; it is an act of immense strength. It takes an extraordinary kind of courage to release someone from the hold of our anger, especially when every part of us cries out for justice. Kush could have let bitterness consume him, choosing the path of revenge. But he chose something far greater - he chose peace. And in that choice, he found freedom, releasing himself from the heavy chains of his own grief.

Revenge and forgiveness are two sides of the same coin. Revenge might give us a fleeting sense of satisfaction, a brief moment where we feel like we've balanced the scales. But deep down, it rarely fills the emptiness or brings the peace we long for. On the other hand, forgiveness is not easy - it asks us to look beyond our hurt, to release the grip of anger, and to let go of the need to make others suffer for their wrongs. But in doing so, it gives us something far more valuable: the ability to reclaim our own peace and strength. Kush, through his journey, realized that true peace doesn't come from trying to control others or seeking justice on our terms. It comes from mastering ourselves, from understanding that the power to heal lies in how we choose to respond, not in how we try to force the world to change.

There will be moments in life when it feels like the world has turned against us, when the weight of betrayal leaves us struggling to breathe. In those times, a wave of anger might rise within us, pushing us to think, "How could you do this to me? Now, I'll show you just how much it hurts." But in those moments, it's important to remember that revenge, as tempting as it may seem, only keeps us tied to the very people who have caused us pain. It doesn't heal us; it only drags us deeper into the darkness. Forgiveness, however, is the key that releases us from that grip. It frees us from the hurt and allows us to move forward. After all, if you choose to make them feel what they made you feel, how are you any different from them?

Much like Arjun standing on the battlefield, torn between his duty and his emotions, we too must learn the difference between fighting for what is right and giving in to the fiery urge for revenge. The battle within ourselves can be just as intense, and it's in these moments of anger that we need to step back and choose the path of justice over retribution. And just like Kush, who carried the weight of his grief and struggles, we must find the strength to let go - believing that the universe, in its own way, will take care of what we cannot. In the end, peace is not something we find through the actions of others, but in how we respond. Revenge may seem tempting, but it offers nothing more than a fleeting sense of satisfaction, leaving the heart still restless. For revenge never satisfies.

DARKNESS

Q7. How do I get out of the darkness in my life?

Once in our lifetime, we inevitably encounter a phase of profound darkness. There are times in life when everything feels uncertain. Our career seems unstable, and the relationships we hold dear fail to bring us the peace we so desperately crave. Family, which should be a source of comfort, feels distant, and even being alone with our thoughts becomes overwhelming. Our minds, once calm, are now a chaotic storm of negative thoughts, filled with endless questions that circle without answers - how? why? what if?. In these moments, it's hard not to feel like we are trapped in a situation that feels unfair, like we've been handed a burden we didn't deserve. No matter where we turn - whether it's the familiarity of our own home or the supposed sanctuary of a temple - we can't seem to find the peace we seek. The weight of it all presses in, and we wonder if there's any way out.

The mind is constantly bombarded with questions. Especially when life hasn't yet aligned with our dreams - career feels stuck, financial growth is negligible, you remain unmarried or without a companion, and your friends seem to have it all figured out. The comparisons we make with others only intensify, especially with the curated successes displayed on social media. These comparisons become a relentless burden because nowadays, we open our phones even before we fully open our eyes. The first glimpse of someone's life seems to set a frustrating tone for the day: "He got married," "She just had a baby," "She landed that dream job at NASA," "He bought a new Mustang," or "She moved to the USA." Meanwhile, you may still be struggling to find stability, despite your many talents. Success should never be bound by age or time, as each of us follows a unique timeline. Consider how Colonel Sanders achieved success with KFC in his 60s, while Mark Zuckerberg founded Facebook at just 19. Both journeys are equally valid, reminding us that there is no set schedule for success.

Social media, in itself, isn't inherently harmful, but it has a way of quietly encouraging us to measure ourselves against others. Even those of us who try to brush off the opinions of others aren't completely shielded from its influence. Sure, social media has its perks - connecting us with people, sharing ideas, and even sparking creativity - but it subtly molds the way we think, often without us realizing it. A little comparison now and then is part of life, and it can even push us to do better. But when that comparison becomes constant, unchecked, it can start to wear us down. What might begin as innocent self-reflection can turn into self-criticism, leading us into a spiral of self-doubt. Slowly, we begin to believe that we're not enough, and that sense of inadequacy takes root, making everything feel a little heavier with each passing day.

In Search of Her Own Sky

Avni, a lively 23-year-old science student and a dedicated badminton player, had always dreamed of advancing in her favorite sport. Her hard work paid off when she reached the national level, a milestone that filled her with pride and hope for the future. But after graduation, everything changed. Her family, who once supported her dreams, now urged her to abandon her athletic aspirations and focus on pursuing a master's degree. The weight of their expectations crushed her spirit.

She felt as though the very thing that had given her life meaning was now slipping away. Her heart ached with each passing day, knowing that the path she had envisioned for herself was slipping through her fingers. But it wasn't just her athletic journey that was faltering. Her friendships, once full of laughter and shared dreams, began to fall apart. The connections that had once given her comfort and strength now felt distant, leaving her feeling isolated and alone.

As the days turned into weeks, she found herself adrift in a sea of uncertainty. The excitement and passion that once fueled her seemed to vanish. In its place was an emptiness that made everything feel meaningless. She spent hours scrolling through social media, watching the world around her move forward while she stood still. Friends were finding love, chasing their passions, and celebrating milestones, while she felt as if she was fading into the background, unable to keep up. The more she watched, the deeper the ache in her chest grew, until she wondered if she'd ever find her way back to the person she used to be.

As time went on, loneliness consumed her more and more. The sense of being powerless over her own life began to crush her spirit - her dreams, once full of promise, now lay forgotten, and her relationships, strained beyond recognition, only added to her pain. She found solace in solitude, spending endless days shut away in her room, drowning in her own thoughts. Even when she managed to step outside, surrounded by family or friends, her mind remained trapped in an endless cycle of sadness and frustration. The constant comparisons to others only deepened her sorrow, pulling her into a dark place where hope seemed like a distant memory. Despite all her attempts to escape the darkness, the thought lingered relentlessly: "My life is over; there's nothing left to live for."

Though nothing catastrophic had happened - her career had simply taken a different turn, and personal setbacks had left their mark - the weight of unfulfilled dreams hung over her like a shadow. The expectations she had set for herself felt like an unrelenting pressure, and the strain soon began to show in every part of her being. Her body grew tired; she lost weight, and her once-lustrous hair became thinner with each passing day. Anxiety crept into her thoughts, and low blood pressure became an all-too-familiar feeling at this very young age. But more than anything, what Avni craved was not just someone to lean on, but the strength to believe in herself once more. She needed the courage to step forward, to look at the road ahead and see it not as a dead end, but as a chance to start fresh, to redefine her path.

In time, she began to understand the depth of her struggles, and with a quiet but meaningful shift, she took a small step toward healing. She embraced the comfort of books, allowing herself to get lost in stories that nourished her soul, while gradually stepping away from the constant pull of social media. Each time she scrolled, she did so with a new mindset: "May God bless them; I'm moving at my own pace, and that's okay." It wasn't about comparing her journey to others anymore - it was about embracing her own path. The real victory, however, came when she realized she no longer had to be ruled by the endless chatter in her mind. Slowly, she learned to take control, silencing the inner chaos that once dictated her every thought. It wasn't easy, but with each day, she felt stronger - winning a quiet, hard-won battle within herself.

उद्धरेदात्मनात्मानं नात्मानमवसादयेत्।
आत्मैव ह्यात्मनो बन्धुरात्मैव रिपुरात्मन: ॥ 6.5

{One must elevate oneself with the help of the mind and
not degrade oneself. The mind is the friend of the

conditioned soul and its enemy as well.}

Over time, Avni slowly began to rediscover her connection to spirituality, returning to the practices that had once filled her heart with peace. She stumbled upon a mentor through online videos, whose wisdom resonated deeply with her. The preacher's words became a guiding light, bringing a sense of clarity and warmth she hadn't felt in a long while. This guidance sparked something within her - a glimmer of hope, fragile but unmistakable.

As she listened to stories of people who had faced unimaginable struggles and triumphed, Avni felt a shift within herself. She began to see her life not as a race against a ticking clock, but as her own journey, free from the weight of societal expectations. The pressure to meet certain milestones by a specific age began to lose its hold on her, fading like an old fear that no longer made sense. Her healing didn't come overnight, but it started when she realized that it was time to release the burdens of past expectations and redirect her energy toward what truly mattered. She began to reclaim her life, one small step at a time, with a quiet determination to find peace on her own terms.

तद्विद्धि प्रणिपातेन परिप्रश्नेन सेवया।
उपदेक्ष्यन्ति ते ज्ञानिनस्तत्त्वदर्शिनः ॥ 4.34

{Seek the truth by approaching a spiritual master. Inquire with humility and offer service; the wise, having realized the truth, will impart knowledge to you.}

Her practice helped her see things clearly - her goals, her purpose, and the steps needed to get there. The journey wasn't fast, but it was certain. The real victory wasn't in the outward achievements, but in the peace she found within herself.

She got back up on her feet gradually. She transformed her greatest struggle, overthinking, into a powerful resource. No longer overwhelmed by the constant swirl of thoughts, she realized that this very tendency, which once held her captive, could be redirected into something productive. With this shift in perspective, she made the bold decision to pursue law, believing that it was the perfect path to channel her mental energy. Her family, sensing the newfound clarity and determination in her, supported her choice without hesitation, trusting that she had found her true calling. Today, Avni is a successful notary public lawyer in one of India's bustling cities, a living proof of the inner growth she experienced. Her story is a reminder that sometimes, the most meaningful progress happens within.

Life often takes us through challenging phases, much like the one Avni faced, where it feels like everything is in disarray. Yet, the true test lies in gathering the courage to take that first step toward healing. It's easy to forget that our paths are ours alone to walk, and comparing ourselves to others can create unnecessary pressure. Just because someone else finds success early doesn't mean we are failing or falling behind. We often fall into the delusional trap of believing we will never feel the same passion or dedication for one endeavor as we did for another, but this too shall unfold in it's own time. It's important to remind ourselves that our moment will come. What truly matters is staying faithful to our journey, without letting comparisons cloud our vision.

We must also make peace with our minds. When left unchecked, our thoughts can become our greatest adversaries, pulling us deeper into self-doubt and darkness. Even when life feels like a race, and we are tempted to measure our progress against others, it's essential not to let the fear of "falling behind" take away our sense of self. Keep moving forward, one step at a time, trusting in your unique path. Hold on to the belief that the universe has a plan for you, and the same faith that guides you will lead you toward the light.

तेषामेवानुकम्पार्थमहमज्ञानजं तमः।
नाशयाम्यात्मभावस्थो ज्ञानदीपेन भास्वता॥ 10.11

{Out of compassion, I dwell within their hearts

and, with the lamp of knowledge, dispel the darkness born of ignorance.}

The lesson in this story is simple, yet deeply meaningful: True happiness and fulfillment don't come from external achievements or material wealth; they come from within. When we stop seeking joy in what's around us and begin to look inward, we find that contentment grows from a place deep inside. By nurturing our inner awareness and letting our own light shine, we begin to let go of the need for approval from the outside world. Freedom doesn't come from chasing after success or measuring ourselves against others; it comes from finding peace within and aligning with what truly matters to us. The person who learns to live in tune with their inner self rises above the noise and distractions, stepping into a life of clarity and purpose, free from illusions, and walking toward what is right for them.

योऽन्तःसुखोऽन्तरारामस्तथान्तर्ज्योतिरेव यः।
स योगी ब्रह्मनिर्वाणं ब्रह्मभूतोऽधिगच्छति ॥ 5.24

{One whose joy lies within, who finds contentment within, and whose light shines inward is the true mystic. Such a person, liberated from worldly attachments, attains the Supreme.}

When a person finds true contentment within themselves, nothing from the outside world, no matter how tempting or captivating it may seem, can disturb their inner calm. The noise and distractions of the external world lose their grip, and even in the face of allure or chaos, a sense of peace remains anchored deep within. This inner fulfillment acts as a shield, protecting the soul from the baseless distractions that might otherwise stir restlessness.

KNOWLEDGE

Q8. What is the difference between education and knowledge? Is being knowledgeable above being educated?

In the hustle and bustle of today's world, the words "education" and "knowledge" are often thrown around as if they mean the same thing. This casual interchange can blur the lines between their unique purposes and what they truly represent. Education and knowledge are deeply connected but not identical. Their roles in shaping our lives differ greatly, just as the tools and the wisdom to use them differ.

The Bhagavad Geeta shines a light on this distinction, encouraging us to reflect on the deeper essence of both. Education equips us with skills, facts, and the ability to perform tasks, while knowledge goes beyond - it is the inner awakening that brings clarity, wisdom, and an understanding of the larger truths of life. The two, though intertwined, often lead to entirely different paths, shaping not just what we achieve but how we perceive and live our lives.

Understanding this difference can be transformative. It reminds us that while education might help us excel in the outer world, knowledge enriches the soul, guiding us toward a more meaningful and fulfilled existence. The Bhagavad Geeta offers a gentle yet profound reminder of what it means to truly "know."

Education (शिक्षा - shiksha) is the journey through which a person discovers knowledge, skills, and abilities that shape their future. It unfolds in structured spaces like schools and universities, where young minds are molded and guided through various disciplines. These settings are not just about learning facts or mastering formulas; they are spaces where curiosity is nurtured, creativity is encouraged, and the foundations for a meaningful life are laid.

At its heart, education is about much more than textbooks and exams. It sharpens the mind to think critically, solve problems, and make informed decisions. It empowers individuals to explore their potential and equips them with the tools to pursue dreams and face challenges. Education plays a crucial role in preparing individuals for specific roles in society, enabling them to contribute to their community while securing their livelihood.

Through this process, a child learns not just to survive but to thrive - growing into someone who can support themselves while also finding purpose and fulfillment in their chosen path.

In contrast, Knowledge (ज्ञान - gyan) goes far beyond the boundaries of academic learning or memorized facts. It is a deep reservoir of wisdom, awareness, and understanding that touches the very essence of life. It's not just about acquiring information but also about gaining insights into what it means to be human - our emotions, values, and the moral compass that guides us.

This kind of knowledge speaks to the heart as much as the mind. It helps us discern right from wrong, understand the complexities of relationships, and make choices that shape who we are. It molds our character, inspiring us to grow not only as individuals but also as compassionate and thoughtful beings. Ultimately, it opens the doors to understanding ourselves and our connection to the greater world, revealing a path to live with a higher purpose.

True knowledge shapes not just the intellect but also the heart, instilling the grace and kindness needed to treat others with dignity and care. It deepens our understanding of what it means to connect with another soul, teaching us the value of empathy and the shared responsibility we hold toward one another. In a world where relationships often risk becoming shallow and driven by personal gain, knowledge becomes a guiding light, inspiring us to see others not as stepping stones or resources, but as companions walking the same path of existence. It transforms how we engage with one another, enriching bonds with genuine respect and a heartfelt sense of humanity.

A timeless instance, in the simplest terms, Ravana, with his boundless intellect and remarkable achievements, stood as a symbol of education and scholarly pursuits. He was a man who had mastered the arts, sciences, and scriptures, his mind vast and brimming with discoveries. On the other hand, Lord Ram, even with all his possessions and royal stature, embodied the essence of true wisdom. His understanding wasn't just intellectual; it resonated in his actions, his values, and his unshakable sense of righteousness.

In today's fast-paced world, society often ties the idea of intelligence to the degrees or formal accolades a person accumulates. This creates a narrow perception that academic success is synonymous with true understanding. But does a certificate truly reflect a person's ability to navigate the human experience? Education, while undeniably valuable for building careers and mastering technical skills, seldom delves into the art of being - of fostering kindness, empathy, and emotional strength.

A degree might teach you how to crack formulas or craft flawless reports, but it rarely equips you to face life's intricate emotional challenges - the heartbreaks, the uncertainties, the silent battles that demand more than just logic. True wisdom doesn't reside in lecture halls or printed syllabi; it emerges in those quiet, raw moments when life tests your patience, compassion, and inner strength. These are the lessons that shape who we are, molding us into individuals who understand that wisdom is as much about the heart as it is about the mind.

Through my experiences with a diverse range of

professionals - whether it be commissioners, surgeons, bureaucrats, or artists - I've observed something unsettling. Despite their impressive educational achievements, many individuals still find themselves entangled in moments where their actions towards their own families reflect a deep disregard for ethics and empathy. It's a troubling contradiction. It brings to light that knowledge and degrees alone cannot define a person's true character or their ability to nurture relationships. Education may shape the mind, but it is the heart, the choices we make, and the way we treat others that truly speak to who we are. This stark reality serves as a reminder that the heart cannot be taught in classrooms, and some lessons in life are learned far beyond textbooks.

अमानित्वमदम्भित्वमहिंसा क्षान्तिरार्जवम् |

आचार्योपासनं शौचं स्थैर्यमात्मविनिग्रहः || 8||

इन्द्रियार्थेषु वैराग्यमनहङ्कार एव च |

जन्ममृत्युजराव्याधिदुःखदोषानुदर्शनम् || 9||

असक्तिरनभिष्वङ्गः पुत्रदारगृहादिषु |

नित्यं च समचित्तत्वमिष्टानिष्टोपपत्तिषु || 10||

मयि चानन्ययोगेन भक्तिरव्यभिचारिणी |

विविक्तदेशसेवित्वमरतिर्जनसंसदि || 11||

अध्यात्मज्ञाननित्यत्वं तत्वज्ञानार्थदर्शनम् |
एतज्ज्ञानमिति प्रोक्तमज्ञानं यदतोऽन्यथा || 12||

{Humility, pridelessness; nonviolence; tolerance; simplicity; approaching a bona fide spiritual master; cleanliness; steadiness; self-control; renunciation of the objects of sense gratification; absence of false ego; the perception of the evil of birth, death, old age and disease; detachment; freedom from entanglement with children, wife, home and the rest; even-mindedness amid pleasant and unpleasant events; constant and unalloyed devotion to Me; aspiring to live a solitary place; detachment from the general mass of people; accepting the importance of self-realization; and philosophical search for the Absolute Truth - all these I declare to be knowledge, and besides this whatever there may be is ignorance.}

This verse beautifully highlights that true wisdom goes beyond the lessons we learn in school. It teaches us that qualities like humility, kindness, patience, and devotion hold the key to understanding life on a deeper level. These traits shape our character and guide us toward a more meaningful existence, leading us to act with compassion and integrity. Unlike what formal education may offer, they are the unseen foundations of a person's soul - softly steering them toward a life filled with purpose and connection. These values nurture a sense of responsibility, making us more aware of our actions and how they impact the world around us.

Knowledge rooted in compassion forms the very core of how we connect with others. It shapes the way we treat people, instilling a sense of kindness and respect that is essential for building strong, meaningful relationships. When we learn through compassion, we begin to understand the importance of truly listening to those around us, not just hearing their words but feeling their emotions and intentions. It teaches us to engage with others in a way that is caring and present, offering support without judgment. In doing so, we see the invisible threads that bind us all, reminding us that we are never truly alone. This kind of knowledge helps us build connections that go beyond surface-level interactions, allowing us to be a positive influence in the lives of others and in the world around us.

द्रव्ययज्ञास्तपोयज्ञा योगयज्ञास्तथापरे।

स्वाध्यायज्ञानयज्ञाश्च यतयः संशितव्रताः ॥ 4.28

{Having accepted strict vows, some become enlightened by sacrificing their possessions, and others by performing severe austerities, by practicing the yoga of eightfold mysticism, or by studying the Vedas to advance in transcendental knowledge.}

Here, different paths to knowledge are acknowledged, emphasizing that education should facilitate self-discovery and spiritual awakening. It should empower individuals to question, seek wisdom, and cultivate a deeper understanding of their existence.

True knowledge allows individuals to recognize the innate worth of all beings, teaching them the importance of kindness, patience, and integrity in their interactions. When education encourages the pursuit of such knowledge, it becomes a transformative force in shaping individuals who are not only skilled in their professions but also compassionate in their personal lives. In the end what's the point of such degrees that couldn't teach a man to respect his partner?

However, in the contemporary world, there's a growing trend where formal education takes precedence over the development of a person's character and values. We see so many caught up in the race for degrees, titles, and achievements, all the while forgetting the deeper, more meaningful parts of life. This chase often blinds individuals to what truly matters - the ability to feel for others, to listen with kindness, and to share in the joys and struggles of those around us. When we become too focused on success and recognition, we lose sight of the compassion, empathy, and understanding that make us truly human. Without these qualities, it becomes harder to connect with one another, and the bonds that hold society together begin to weaken.

श्रेयान्द्रव्यमयाद्यज्ञाज्ज्ञानयज्ञः परन्तप।

सर्वं कर्माखिलं पार्थ ज्ञाने परिसमाप्यते॥ 4.33

{O chastiser of the enemy, the sacrifice performed in knowledge is better than the mere sacrifice of material possessions. After all, O son of Prtha, all sacrifices of action culminate in transcendental knowledge.}

Education, often defined by formal schooling and the acquisition of skills, primarily equips individuals with information necessary for career development. In contrast, knowledge transcends this foundation; it embodies wisdom, understanding, and the ability to apply insights in real-life situations. This verse emphasizes that true sacrifice lies not in the material offerings we make, but in our commitment to seeking and sharing knowledge. It is through knowledge that we foster moral responsibility and meaningful relationships, ultimately leading to a more enlightened and compassionate society.

इति गुह्यतमं शास्त्रमिदमुक्तं मयानघ |

एतद्बुद्ध्वा बुद्धिमान्स्यात्कृतकृत्यश्च भारत || 20||

{I am the sacred science, the sacred knowledge, the purest

knowledge, and I am that which is the ultimate truth.}

Here, the emphasis is on the importance of pursuing knowledge that leads to understanding the deeper truths of existence. Such knowledge is transformative; it shapes one's values, influences behavior, and fosters a sense of unity with others. When knowledge is rooted in ethical principles, it not only informs one's understanding of life but also dictates how one interacts with others, ensuring that compassion and respect are at the forefront of all relationships.

True knowledge nurtures the understanding that every action has repercussions, encouraging individuals to treat others with kindness and dignity. In this way, knowledge becomes a crucial component in developing the manners necessary for treating others ethically and compassionately. A well-rounded individual is one who recognizes the value of both aspects - utilizing education as a means to gain knowledge while simultaneously embodying the ethical principles outlined in the Geeta.

In today's world, where information is readily available, the challenge lies in discerning valuable knowledge from mere data. The Bhagavad Geeta encourages individuals to cultivate discernment (विवेक), enabling them to differentiate between temporary satisfaction derived from material pursuits and the lasting fulfillment that comes from knowledge.

The differentiation between education and knowledge is crucial for personal and societal growth. Education provides a structured pathway to gain information and skills, while knowledge encompasses a deeper understanding of ethical living, self-realization, and spiritual growth. The Bhagavad Geeta offers timeless wisdom that highlights the importance of cultivating virtuous qualities, reminding us that true knowledge extends beyond the confines of formal education.

Our delicate lives in this complex world, makes it essential to strive for a balance between education and knowledge. By prioritizing ethical principles and cultivating a deeper understanding of ourselves and our surroundings, we can create a more harmonious society where education serves as a tool for enlightenment rather than merely a means to an end. In doing so, we honor the teachings of the Geeta and work toward a future where knowledge leads us to a life of purpose, fulfillment, and unity. Knowledge becomes not just a pursuit of personal achievement but a guiding force that teaches us the manners in which to treat others with kindness and respect, thus enriching both our lives and the lives of those around us. Simply, an illiterate person can be knowledgeable but a literally loaded personality may not always possess true wisdom.

REWARDS

Q9. What is the significance of yagya (sacrifice), tap (penance), and daan (charity) in our modern lives?

To spark interest, let me first address an essential concept: the spiritual significance of "Kaliyug." According to many saints and revered scriptures, this age - despite its association with chaos and decay - holds immense potential for spiritual growth. Among the four epochs (Satya, Treta, Dwapara, and Kaliyug), Kaliyug is considered the most advantageous for achieving divine fruits. What makes Kaliyug stand out is its accelerated effect; the rewards of spiritual actions performed in this age are said to be multiplied tenfold compared to earlier ages. In Satya Yug, achieving liberation demanded excruciating efforts and unwavering discipline. In Treta and Dwapar Yug, too, practitioners had to endure immense hardship and long wait periods to experience the results of their spiritual pursuits. Yet, in Kaliyug, the same fruits can be attained with far less effort, provided one follows the right path with sincerity. This very notion should encourage us to dive into spiritual practices with eagerness, knowing that the path to spiritual rewards has never been more accessible.

Yagya: A Forgotten Habit of Divine Balance

"Yagya" is perhaps one of the most familiar terms in Hindu tradition, yet it has faded into obscurity, misunderstood by many and dismissed by others. I hesitate to call it merely a "ritual." Instead, it is a habit - a sacred practice that ought to become an integral part of our daily lives, as emphasized earlier.

Yagya is far more than an offering to the divine; it serves humanity on a deeper, even scientific level. Yet, in modern times, it is often ridiculed as superstitious - an act that "wastes" essential resources like ghee, wood, and grains (Chaube et al. 2020). This shallow perspective overlooks the fact that yagya is an ancient practice deeply rooted in promoting human welfare. It was never intended to be frivolous, despite being misrepresented as such by some detractors.

One astonishing incident from recent history beautifully illustrates the profound impact of yagya. The 1984 Bhopal gas tragedy remains one of India's darkest moments, with over 3,500 people perishing and countless others left with lifelong disabilities. In the heart of the disaster-stricken area, however, there was one miraculous exception. While thousands struggled for their lives, one family survived unharmed. They had no idea about the poisonous gas leak ravaging their surroundings because, at that very moment, they were immersed in performing Agnihotra Yagya ("How Agnihotra saved a family from Bhopal Gas Tragedy ?" 2012).

This sacred fire ritual involves offerings such as cow dung cakes, camphor, medicinal herbs, seeds, and wood, accompanied by the chanting of prescribed mantras at precise times (muhurat). The aromatic chemicals released during the yagya created an atmosphere that neutralized the deadly effects of methyl isocyanate gas. This incident is more than a miracle - it exemplifies the potent, scientifically-backed benefits of yagya.

Yagya is not merely a spiritual ceremony; it offers protection and fosters inner peace. Once a person experiences the serenity and divine aura it brings, the practice becomes almost addictive, drawing the practitioner deeper into spiritual devotion. In the *Bhagavad Geeta*, Lord Krishn emphasizes that yagya cleanses the soul of karmic impurities, setting the performer on a path of liberation. Whether the yagya is Nishkaam (performed without desire) or Sakaam (aimed at fulfilling a desire), it yields corresponding results.

सर्वेऽप्येते यज्ञविदो यज्ञक्षपितकल्मषा:।
यज्ञशिष्टामृतभुजो यान्ति ब्रह्म सनातनम्।। 4.30

(All those who understand the meaning of sacrifice become free from sins and, having tasted the nectar of its fruits, advance toward the eternal divine realm.)

However, yagya is not a shortcut to divine grace. Many people hope that performing rituals will miraculously erase their karmic burdens, as if salvation is a product they can purchase at will. We often fail to grasp that our lives revolve around cycles of karma, endlessly fueled by our own actions. Yet, instead of striving for liberation, we remain entangled in material desires. How ironic it is - when offered a chance to dissolve karmic debts, the fickle mind still craves houses, cars, and luxuries. The soul, trapped within the body's insatiable greed, struggles to seek peace beyond worldly pleasures.

Beyond its role in cleansing karma, yagya possesses supernatural powers that extend far beyond this material world. It is said that yagya can summon rains during droughts, stop storms, heal diseases, or bring forth prosperity from barren lands. Wars have been won, oceans stilled, and deserts cultivated through the divine force of yagya. Whether it is performed for marriage, fertility, wealth, or spiritual awakening, the possibilities are boundless. Such is the transformative power of yagya.

Though its effects are awe-inspiring, yagya is not

something to be taken lightly. Curiosity may inspire some to begin performing yagyas, but it is essential to understand the precision required. Yagya, when performed incorrectly - with the wrong ingredients, improper mantras, or at unsuitable times - can yield no results or even have negative consequences. For a yagya to reach the divine and bear fruit, it must align perfectly with the guidelines laid out in the Vedas. A poorly executed yagya becomes Tamasik - in the mode of ignorance - creating unintended disruptions rather than harmony.

विधिहीनमसृष्टान्नं मन्त्रहीनमदक्षिणम्।
श्रद्धाविरहितं यज्ञं तामसं परिचक्षते॥ 17.13

{A sacrifice that disregards scriptural
instructions, lacks appropriate offerings, or is
performed without faith, is considered to be in
the mode of ignorance.}

It is essential to approach yagya with reverence, care, and awareness. Even the smallest misstep - using the wrong herbs, chanting mantras incorrectly, or performing it in the wrong season - can disrupt its intended outcome. When not done with devotion and precision, the yagya becomes ineffective, and instead of purifying, it may introduce doshas (imbalances) into the performer's life.

To engage with yagya is to walk a path toward both worldly well-being and spiritual transcendence. It invites us to step beyond our material cravings and connect with the divine forces that govern the universe. It teaches us that life is not only about fulfilling physical desires but about nourishing the soul. The fire of yagya does not merely burn wood - it burns away ignorance, purifies intentions, and transforms karma, offering us a glimpse of something eternal. Without yagya, happiness remains elusive - here and beyond.

Penance: A Journey Through Time and Self

Once, in the ancient age of *Treta Yug*, exceptional individuals embraced penance as a powerful means to fulfill their desires and attain supernatural powers. These tales of penance are woven into the stories of Indian mythology, capturing our imaginations. It is said that demons, too, engaged in intense penance, seeking favorable boons from the deities. This arduous journey often spanned years, with ascetics holding steadfast to their postures, renouncing food, water, and shelter while reciting sacred mantras, sometimes standing on one foot.

Take, for instance, Hiranyakashipu, who, after enduring relentless penance, received a boon of immortality from Lord Brahma. This boon rendered him nearly invincible - neither to be killed during the day nor at night, neither inside nor outside, and by neither man nor beast, nor with any weapon. Another poignant tale features Sage Atri and his devoted wife. Distressed by the suffering caused by a terrible drought, they adopted penance, during which the sage's wife served the deities with unwavering faith while the sage sat for a penance. Their devotion manifested the holy river Ganga along with other rivers, bringing much-needed relief to the parched earth. Thus, penance can be undertaken with both noble and ignoble intentions.

In our current age of *Kaliyug*, it is vital that we adapt our practice of penance to resonate with the modern world. While the penance of *Treta* and *Dwapar Yug* was undoubtedly rigorous, today we have easier access to embrace a form of penance that suits our times. Our world often lacks fundamental qualities such as kindness, love, equality, respect, and sharing. Therefore, it is essential for us, to some extent, to adopt this modern approach to penance - an idea echoed not only in ancient scriptures but also imparted by the greatest sages and gurus throughout history.

I refer to this modern approach as both effortless and yet profoundly challenging, particularly due to the fickleness of our minds. Ironically, this form of penance is the simplest among all four yugas, which is why ancient sages regarded *Kaliyug* as the best age for spiritual advancement. We can contemplate three primary forms of penance in our daily lives.

The first form emphasizes physical discipline, wherein individuals free themselves from self-indulgence and dedicate their body, mind, and spirit to serving elders, teachers, and the Supreme. Throughout history, we have seen countless individuals, young and old, commit themselves to this path, more commonly within communities like ISKCON, Jainism, and Buddhism. This commitment involves not just heartfelt service but also a sincere effort to lead a simple and harmonious life, often referred to as a *sattvik* (pure and simple) lifestyle. However, in today's fast-paced world, few choose to embrace this path of peace and coherence.

देवद्विजगुरुप्राज्ञपूजनं शौचमार्जवम्।
ब्रह्मचर्यमहिंसा च शारीरं तप उच्यते॥ 17.14

{Austerity of the body consists in worship of the Supreme Lord, the brahmanas, the spiritual masters, and superiors like father and mother, and in cleanliness, simplicity, celibacy, and nonviolence.}

The second form of penance encourages us to refrain from abusing others. Many mistakenly believe that dominating those of lesser status demonstrates strength or masculinity. But, in truth, such behavior only reveals our own weaknesses. It is a feeble mind that feels compelled to offend others to gain a fleeting sense of superiority. Conversely, kindness costs us nothing; no one ever loses by being kind. This goodwill should extend beyond the less fortunate to our colleagues, family members, and loved ones. If one cannot speak kindly, it is far better to remain silent than to spread negativity.

Moreover, it is not enough to merely utter kind words; we must also strive to speak truthfully. Embracing honesty in every situation benefits both ourselves and those around us, providing clarity for them and peace for us. There is a profound relief in not having to remember the multitude of lies concocted to maintain a façade. This liberation from deceit is perhaps the greatest advantage of truthfulness. When we lie, we clutter our minds with the burden of cover-ups, perpetually anxious about being discovered. Even the slightest hint of apprehension can lead to fear, ensnaring our thoughts in a web of deceit. The beauty of being truthful lies in the simplicity of memory; when we speak honestly, we carry no weight of falsehood, allowing our minds to remain at ease, accompanied by the satisfaction of living in alignment with our true selves.

Additionally, the pursuit of truth reveals a crucial insight: when we lie, we may fool others temporarily, feeling clever in our deception. Yet, deep down, we are aware of our wrongdoing, and there is always a higher power observing our actions. Whether we acknowledge it or not, the Supreme is perpetually watching us.

अनुद्वेगकरं वाक्यं सत्यं प्रियहितं च यत्।
स्वाध्यायाभ्यसनं चैव वाङ्मयं तप उच्यते ॥ 17.15

{Austerity of speech consists in speaking words that are truthful, pleasing, beneficial, and not aGeetating to others, and also in regularly reciting Vedic literature.}

Among these three forms of penance, the most challenging is the penance of the mind. Our minds can be our greatest adversary or our truest ally, yet mastering them can feel like an insurmountable task. This mental penance begins with self-satisfaction. A man who is content with himself and his reality is truly powerful. This does not mean he refrains from pursuing his desires; rather, it signifies that he is free from material cravings. Such a man finds fulfillment in what God has already bestowed upon him, nurturing unwavering faith in the divine plan that unfolds at its own pace. In this journey, seeking the Supreme becomes his only true desire.

Another admirable quality of those who undertake this mental penance is their inherent simplicity. This simplicity permeates every aspect of life - lifestyle, clothing, speech, and perspective - creating a holistic approach rather than focusing on any one particular aspect. It is important to clarify that following this path does not necessitate abandoning the material world; instead, it calls for such self-control over our minds that the distractions of materialism cannot deter us from our ultimate goal - becoming one with the divine.

मनःप्रसादः सौम्यत्वं मौनमात्मविनिग्रहः।
भावसंशुद्धिरित्येतत्तपो मानसमुच्यते ॥ 17.16

{And satisfaction, simplicity, gravity, self-control, and

purification of one's existence are the austerities of the mind.}

Now, one might question, "What material outcomes can we expect from such penance?" The fruits of penance transcend our immediate desires, offering us even more than we dare to dream. The discipline and mindset cultivated through penance lead us closer to God after we have experienced the pleasures of materialism. We begin to recognize that the material world is but a fleeting trap. However, before embarking on this journey, one must adhere to certain principles.

First and foremost, clarity and intention are essential. We should not enter this practice expecting tangible rewards; rather, we must accept it as a lifestyle and a form of service to God. In essence, penance should not be viewed as a means to fulfill our desires, as it once was in earlier ages. I urge against using it solely as a method for wish fulfillment, for numerous other avenues exist for that purpose. It is wiser to embrace penance as a transformative lifestyle for personal growth, which ultimately serves as our highest aim. By practicing self-discipline and devotion to God, we open ourselves to receiving gifts beyond our imagination. Such is the greatness of the Divine. Yet, we must ensure our devotion is free from the greed of return, for the Supreme sees through our intentions. Thus, only penance performed without expectation is considered pure.

श्रद्धया परया तप्तं तपस्तत्त्रिविधं नरैः।
अफलाकाङ्क्षिभिरयुक्तैः सात्त्विकं परिचक्षते ॥ 17.17

{This threefold austerity, performed with transcendental faith by men not expecting material benefits but engaged only for the sake of the Supreme, is called austerity in goodness.}

Moreover, those who embark on such austerity with an underlying desire for fruit, while harboring an egoistic mindset, miss the essence of the practice. Such individuals may see their penance as a competition, attempting to satisfy their spiritual egos. However, this approach fails to connect with the Divine, for God yearns for love, not pretense. Thus, one must refrain from engaging in austerity with spiritual arrogance or a desire to display one's piety to the world.

सत्कारमानपूजार्थं तपो दम्भेन चैव यत्।
क्रियते तदिह प्रोक्तं राजसं चलमध्रुवम् ॥ 17.18

{Penance performed out of pride and for the sake of gaining respect, honor, and worship is said to be in the mode of passion. It is neither stable nor permanent.}

Lastly, those who are physically or mentally incapable of undertaking such rigorous practices yet insist on pursuing them, whether out of goodness or malice, engage in self-harm according to scripture. This foolishness leads nowhere; it brings neither spiritual benefit nor discipline but rather results in harm to oneself, ultimately leading to mental and physical decay.

मूढग्राहेणात्मनो यत्पीडया क्रियते तपः।

परस्योत्सादनार्थं वा तत्तामसमुदाहृतम्॥ 17.19

{Penance performed out of foolishness, with self-torture or to destroy or injure others, is said to be in the mode of ignorance.}

Charity: The Art of Selfless Giving

In the flow of human life, charity binds compassion and empathy into something meaningful. Throughout our journeys, many of us encounter astrologers who reveal that certain planets in our charts may carry malefic influences. As a remedy for these perceived misfortunes, they often suggest acts of donation - be it clothes, groceries, or other essentials. This practice has influenced our collective mindset, leading many to believe that acts of charity should only occur during personal crises or troubles. Expectation has, in a sense, become a human default, creating a transactional lens through which we view giving. However, if we could shift this mindset, we could spark profound changes within ourselves and the society.

Have you ever pondered what might happen if the wealthy members of society dedicated even a small portion of their wealth to uplift the less fortunate? Imagine a world where everyone has access to two meals a day and a roof over their heads. The vision is alluring, yet it remains a distant ideal, seldom manifested in reality. Often, we are quick to dismiss the struggles of others, thinking that someone else will bear the burden of change. While the landscape may seem bleak, it is essential to recognize that exceptions do exist - individuals and organizations genuinely committed to making a difference in the lives of others.

In our contemporary world, the act of charity often comes with a desire for recognition. Some individuals, upon donating, feel an insatiable need to capture the moment, snapping photos for newspapers or sharing their good deeds on social media platforms. While it is commendable that they engage in acts of kindness, it is equally crucial to delve deeper into the motivations behind these donations. Are we giving to elevate our own status, or are we truly aiming to make a lasting impact on someone else's life?

The true essence of charity lies in providing for those in need without the expectation of reward. It is not merely about giving; it is about ensuring that our donations reach the right person, at the right time, and in the right place. This authentic form of charity, as described in our scriptures, transcends transactional gestures. It reflects our humanity, bridging the gap between different segments of society and paving the way toward a more equitable world.

In many Indian households, when individuals no longer wish to use their clothes or utensils, they often choose to donate them to those in need. However, they frequently overlook a crucial reality: many of these items are sorted, with the better-quality goods resold. This commodification of charity raises ethical questions: Are we genuinely helping, or are we simply clearing out our closets while feeling good about ourselves?

For instance, let us consider the well-meaning individuals who donate blankets and warm clothing to the homeless. They believe they are alleviating suffering, yet some of these individuals may choose to sell the very items intended to keep them warm, opting instead to sleep bare in the bitter cold. This disheartening reality highlights a fundamental issue: the disconnect between the giver and the receiver. When we neglect to understand the needs of those we aim to assist, we risk undermining the very purpose of our generosity.

Similarly, consider the scenario where we give cash to an elderly beggar, intending for them to purchase a meal. It is disheartening to discover that they might choose to spend it on alcohol instead. These scenarios illustrate the all-too-common instances where charity inadvertently goes awry, leaving us questioning the effectiveness of our efforts. Such acts do not yield positive karma; instead, they often contribute to a reservoir of negative karma though your intention was pure but only because you became a medium to his bad karma. Because Karma is circular. Therefore, it is crucial to ensure that our donations reach those genuinely in need - such as NGOs that rescue animals, government schools supporting underprivileged students, or organizations facilitating the marriages of those in need. These entities possess a better understanding of how to channel resources effectively, ensuring that help reaches those who require it the most.

So, the next time you consider donating or offering assistance, take a moment to reflect on your intentions. Are you genuinely trying to help, or do you secretly hope for something in return? Are you driven by a desire to impress those around you? Reflect on whether your charity is truly reaching those who need it. As I mentioned earlier, God is always observing our actions, keeping track of our deeds. Ultimately, who do we truly need to impress?

Moreover, the act of charity should stem from a place of love and compassion. It is essential to cultivate a mindset that values the well-being of others as an intrinsic part of our existence. When we begin to view charity not as a chore or a transaction but as a privilege, our approach shifts dramatically. Each act of giving becomes an opportunity to connect with others, to understand their struggles, and to contribute to their journey toward a better life.

In this context, we can explore various forms of charity that resonate with our personal values and beliefs. For example, volunteering our time at local shelters, food banks, or community centers allows us to engage directly with those in need. This hands-on approach fosters genuine connections and provides insight into the challenges faced by marginalized individuals. Rather than simply donating items or money, we become active participants in the lives of those we aim to help, enhancing our understanding of their circumstances.

दातव्यमिति यदानं दीयतेऽनुपकारिणे।
देशे काले च पात्रे च तद्दानं सात्त्विकं स्मृतम्॥ 17.20

{Charity given out of duty, without expectation of return, at the proper time and place, and to a worthy person is considered to be in the mode of goodness.}

This perspective transforms charity from an obligation into a profound act of service. It encourages us to look beyond ourselves and our circumstances, fostering a sense of community and shared responsibility. When we approach our acts of giving with eyes open, we not only improve the lives of those around us but also contribute to our own spiritual growth.

As we engage in charity, it becomes imperative to evaluate the systems and structures that perpetuate inequality and suffering. Addressing root causes requires us to examine the socio-economic conditions that create disparities. Supporting initiatives that advocate for systemic change, whether through education, policy reform, or grassroots activism, empowers us to contribute to a more equitable society. It is not enough to provide temporary relief; we must also strive to create lasting solutions.

एतान्यपि तु कर्माणि सङ्खं त्यक्त्वा फलानि च।
कर्तव्यानीति मे पार्थ निश्चितं मतमुत्तमम्॥ 18.6

{All these activities should be performed without attachment or any expectations of result. They should be performed as a matter of duty, O son of Prtha. That is my final opinion.}

Ultimately, the heart of charity lies in selflessness and a genuine desire to uplift others. When we approach our acts of giving with an open heart and a clear mind, we improve the lives of those we help and contribute to our own spiritual growth. In a world where we often find ourselves caught in cycles of materialism and self-interest, let us strive to embody the true spirit of charity - one that is rooted in love, compassion, and an unwavering commitment to the welfare of all.

As we walk through life, let us remember that charity is not a destination but a continuous journey. Each act of kindness, however small, contributes to a wave that can lead to transformative change. By cultivating a spirit of generosity in our daily lives, we not only uplift those in need but also inspire others to join us in this essential mission. Together, we can create a world where compassion reigns, and the true essence of charity flourishes.

Let us carry forth the understanding that the most meaningful acts of charity are those rooted in authenticity and love. When we give from the heart, without the shadow of expectation, we align ourselves with a higher purpose -

one that transcends individual needs and reminds us of our place in the bigger picture of humanity. As we extend our hands to help others, we simultaneously lift our own spirits, fostering a sense of interconnectedness that is essential for a harmonious world.

TRADITIONS

Q10. What is the importance of Ancestral offerings in our lives? How does it impact us? What are its effects on our lives in modern times as it is avoided considering superstitious?

In our rapidly globalizing world, many are found adopting Western culture at an alarming rate, leading to a disconnection from own roots and the meaningful rituals that have defined our identities for generations. Ancestral offerings, a practice deeply embedded in Hindu tradition, serve as a crucial link to our past and our heritage. As we try balancing our busy lives between work, family, and social obligations, it becomes increasingly easy to dismiss these rituals as outdated or superstitious. However, taking a moment to reflect on their significance can reveal profound benefits that extend beyond mere tradition.

Our great-grandparents practiced specific rituals that were passed down through generations. These traditions were not simply religious obligations; they were acts of reverence, gratitude, and connection to higher powers. The effects of these rituals are not merely historical; they have tangible benefits in our lives today. While many of our parents may have found relative success without fully adhering to these customs, their lives were undoubtedly influenced by the foundational rituals performed by their forebears.

One such ritual, Pindodak Kriya, often referred to as Pind Daan, holds a special place in Hindu traditions. This sacred rite emphasizes the essential bond between the living and their departed ancestors, acting as a bridge that connects generations. At its core, Pindodak Kriya serves a vital purpose: it ensures the peace and liberation of the souls who have passed on, allowing them to ascend to higher realms of existence. The term "Pind" signifies the physical body or form, while "Dak" refers to the offerings made to our ancestors. A central aspect of this ritual involves the preparation and presentation of rice balls - known as pinda - crafted from flour and mixed with ghee and sugar. These offerings symbolize the sustenance provided to the souls of the departed.

Traditionally, families perform Pindodak Kriya during specific times, such as Shraddha ceremonies or Pitr Paksha days, when they gather to pay homage to their ancestors. Engaging in this sacred practice is more than just a ritual; it's a way for individuals to seek the blessings of their forebears. These blessings are believed to enhance the well-being, prosperity, and success of the living family members, with ancestors watching over them and guiding them through life's challenges.

Beyond just blessings, Pindodak Kriya serves as a means to address unresolved karmas within the family lineage. Offering Pind Daan can help alleviate the burdens of past actions that might impact the current generation, facilitating healing and resolution. It reminds us of the sacrifices and efforts made by those who came before us, encouraging gratitude and respect for our family traditions. For many, performing Pindodak Kriya brings a sense of closure regarding the loss of loved ones, allowing families to honor their memories, express their grief, and find comfort in the belief that their ancestors are being cared for and remembered (Nayan 2023).

However, in today's fast-paced world, Pindodak Kriya is often met with skepticism. Many people dismiss it as superstition or view it as outdated, especially as they steer modern life influenced by Western culture. Yet, it's essential to recognize that the essence of this ritual transcends mere superstition. Pindodak Kriya is an invaluable link between generations, reinforcing the importance of honoring our roots and the legacy left by our ancestors. As people increasingly find themselves overwhelmed by life's complexities, they often neglect their spiritual obligations. However, dedicating even a small portion of our busy lives to rituals like Pindodak Kriya can have a profound impact on our mental, emotional, and spiritual well-being. By actively engaging with these traditions, we not only acknowledge the efforts of our ancestors but also create a positive effect that can influence our own lives and the lives of future generations.

Today, we witness a generation grappling with a myriad of challenges - from rising mental health issues, such as anxiety and depression, to a lack of clarity in career paths and purpose. The struggle of modern individuals often contrasts sharply with the lives of our ancestors, who, despite their hardships, seemed to possess a certain stability and clarity that many of us now lack. The reason for this may lie in the spiritual and ancestral connections that we have chosen to overlook.

It's important to recognize that while many individuals may attain wealth and success through sheer hard work, there is often an unseen influence at play. The disparity between those who achieve success effortlessly and those who struggle despite their diligence raises questions about the invisible forces governing our lives. Our ancestors, revered in many cultures as powerful spiritual guides, possess an intrinsic connection to our fate. According to ancient scriptures, the highest to bless and protect are held by our late ancestors, kuldevi - kuldevta, and Ishta devta, and are believed to significantly impact our lives.

In the context of karma, it is believed that the consequences of bad deeds are not always immediate. Instead, they often manifest later, affecting the doer's child. This delay serves a purpose. If the results of one's bad karma were to occur instantly, the individual might be mentally prepared to face the consequences, knowing they had committed a wrongful act. As a result, the impact of the suffering might not be as profound. However, when the burden of bad karma falls upon the doer's child, the pain experienced becomes deeply personal. It feels like the pain arrived with interest. Witnessing their child endure hardship strikes at the heart of the doer, delivering the true and intended weight of the karmic consequence. This perspective emphasizes the interconnectedness of actions and their repercussions, extending beyond the individual to those they hold dear. Just as wealth and fame can be inherited, so too can the burden of bad karma.

पुत्रैः समन्वितं पापं यः प्रियतमा आत्मनः।
वर्षाणां शतानि तानि प्रकटयत्यनुशासनम्॥

{A man reaps the consequences of his sins in his descendants.}

(Manusmriti - 4.172)

Conversely, the effects of good karma often follow a similar principle of delayed fruition, but with a more uplifting outcome. When a person performs acts of virtue or kindness, the reward is sometimes passed on to their child. Instead of receiving the blessings directly, the doer experiences joy and fulfillment by witnessing their child thrive and prosper. This dynamic magnifies the reward, as the happiness derived from seeing loved ones benefit from their good deeds often surpasses the satisfaction of personal gain.

संसारवर्तिनं धर्मं यस्तु पत्यं च मातरं।
निवर्तयेद्धि शोकं स जीवेद्वा तु भवेद्विहम्॥

{The one who performs righteous actions in this world, whether for the welfare of his wife, parents, or others, is carried forward by his actions into future lives, affecting his descendants as well}

(Mahabharata - 1.67.24)

In this way, the principles of karma teach that both our good and bad actions flow through generations. Our choices not only shape our destiny but also impact the lives of those closest to us, reminding us of the profound responsibility we hold in our thoughts, words, and deeds. Whether through the lessons of hardship or the blessings of abundance, karma binds us to a web of interconnected experiences that transcend individual lifetimes.

It is within this framework that the positioning of men and women in our scriptures gains deeper significance. I understand the criticism that the mention of women in the below context might attract, but it's important to delve deeper into the essence of how men and women are positioned in our scriptures. Women have always been revered and placed on a pedestal, whether it's through worship or by being honored with immense respect. Our ancestors viewed women as much more than individuals - they saw them as creators, as nurturers, and as the force that breathes life into what might otherwise remain lifeless - whether it is home or a heart.

This reverence wasn't limited to divine goddesses but extended to women in their earthly roles. It was a woman's touch, her energy, and her care that could transform emptiness into a sanctuary of love and life. This recognition of women's ability to create, nurture, and restore balance emphasizes their elevated position in our traditions - a position rooted in respect and deep understanding of their irreplaceable role in the grand design of existence.

अधर्माभिभवात्कृष्ण प्रदुष्यन्ति कुलस्त्रियः।
स्त्रीषु दुष्टासु वार्ष्णेय जायते वर्णसङ्करः॥ 1.41 ॥

{When irreligion is prominent in the family, O Krishn, the women of the family become polluted, and from the degradation of womanhood, O descendant of Vrsni, comes unwanted progeny.}

The verse warns of the degradation of womanhood in the face of irreligion, underscores the foundational role of women in the family structure. In ancient Indian society, women were not merely caretakers; they were the guardians of cultural values and spiritual traditions. When the spiritual canvas of a family begins to fray, it is often the women who bear the brunt of this decline. Their role as nurturers and educators becomes compromised, leading to a loss of moral direction for future generations. This degradation can manifest in various forms, including the emergence of unwanted progeny - children born into circumstances that may lack the guidance and wisdom needed for a fulfilling life.

In earlier times, women were deeply engrossed in their responsibilities - be it at home, in spiritual practices, or within their social circles. Their days were so consumed with these duties that they had little to no time for unproductive or frivolous activities. However, the modern world has brought about a significant shift. Economic challenges have compelled many women to step into roles where they must support their families not just emotionally but financially.

But independence comes with its price. As women strive to provide financial stability and better opportunities for their families, they often find themselves unable to dedicate time to smaller yet meaningful rituals, such as *pind daan.* These practices, which were once a strict part of our life, are now often overlooked or completely neglected.

A more bitter truth is that the pressure of work, combined with the demands of family life, have created environments where some women, in seeking emotional outlets or relief from stress, form relationships outside their marriages. Such situations inevitably affect the sanctity of marriage, not just on emotional and social levels but spiritually as well and that is when the lineage begins to become polluted.

When a woman follows religious or spiritual practices, it is believed that her subconscious remains pure and in harmony to the divine energy. On the other hand, neglecting religion and distancing oneself from spirituality can cloud the subconscious, creating an inner disconnection. Over time, this disconnection unknowingly pave the way for actions that conflict with both moral and spiritual principles.

In simpler terms, the integration of spiritual practices into daily life helps maintain inner clarity and strength. Without this connection, the pressures of modern life can leave a void that is often filled with choices that lead to further discord.

From a scientific standpoint, when two people come together physically, it is believed that an exchange of energy takes place on multiple levels - physical, mental, emotional, and spiritual. This interaction is not just about the tangible transfer of heat or biochemical responses; it also involves the subtle interplay of their electromagnetic fields, generated by the heart and brain. These fields, according to some interpretations in research journals, resonate with each other, creating a unique energetic bond.

Emotionally, this connection fosters a deep sense of intimacy, as hormones like oxytocin and dopamine are released, leading to feelings of attachment. Mentally, such exchanges can influence mood and thought patterns, leaving a lasting impression on the psyche. Spiritually, physical intimacy creates an imprint or energetic trace that lingers, intertwining the individuals' energies and contributing to their personal growth or emotional struggles, depending on the nature of the relationship.

This perspective, rooted in the metaphorical interpretations of quantum principles, highlights the profound and lasting effects that physical intimacy can have on the human experience. These exchanges go far beyond the physical - resonating through our bodies, minds, and souls in ways that we often don't fully understand. It's enough to explain why unwanted physical contact can disrupt our well-being so intensely, affecting us on multiple levels.

The energy that flows between two people during such interactions isn't just a fleeting sensation; it leaves an imprint on our emotional and spiritual well-being. This helps us understand how a single touch can have lasting consequences on our material and spiritual health. It shows how deeply our bodies are connected to our inner worlds and how physical intimacy can influence our state of being.

This idea blends the science of energy with the emotional and spiritual realities we face, offering insight into how our energy exchanges with others shape us, both positively and negatively, on a deeply personal level (Warren 2024).

When a person engages in physical intimacy outside of the sacred bond of marriage, it can invite disruptive and unwanted energies into their lineage. This mixing of energies has the potential to disrupt the purity of the ancestral line, affecting not only the individual but also the generations that follow. The spiritual and emotional consequences of such actions can ripple through the family tree, impacting the well-being and harmony of future generations. The sanctity of marital intimacy is seen as a means of preserving the balance and integrity of one's lineage, protecting it from external influences that could cause lasting harm.

The scriptures teach us that the lineage of a family is sacred, carrying with it the weight of past deeds and the aspirations of ancestors. When families stray from their spiritual obligations, they not only risk their own well-being but also jeopardize the legacy of their forebears. The verse clearly articulates this connection poignantly, illustrating how the neglect of ancestral offerings can lead to a break in the sacred bond that ties generations together. Without these offerings, the departed ancestors are left without sustenance, resulting in a void that reverberates through time. This neglect manifests in the spiritual decline of the family, where a lack of respect for tradition leads to chaos and suffering.

Moreover, the ritualistic offerings made to our ancestors serve as a form of acknowledgment and gratitude for the sacrifices they made for us. By engaging in these acts, we reinforce a familial bond that transcends time. We may not see the immediate effects, but the continuity of these traditions fosters a sense of stability and belonging. In an era where individualism often takes precedence, the collective identity rooted in ancestral heritage can offer profound comfort and guidance.

The consequences of abandoning these practices manifest in various ways. The struggles faced by the current generation - from mental health issues to relationship difficulties - often find their roots in a lack of spiritual grounding. Our ancestors laid a foundation that, when honored, creates a protective shield around us. By neglecting their legacies, we may inadvertently leave ourselves vulnerable to the chaos of modern life.

Even as educated modern individuals, we sometimes fail to acknowledge the supernatural forces at play in our lives. There is a sense of hubris in believing that our intellect and accomplishments can shield us from the influences of the unseen. A balanced view allows us to appreciate the intersection of rationality and spirituality, recognizing that our lives are not solely dictated by our actions but also by the energies and blessings that surround us.

सङ्करो नरकायैव कुलघ्नानां कुलस्य च।
पतन्ति पितरो ह्येषां लुप्तपिण्डोदकक्रियाः ॥ 1.42 ॥

{An increase in unwanted population certainly causes hellish life for both the family and for those who destroy the family tradition. The ancestors of such corrupt families fall down because the performances of offering them food and water are entirely stopped.}

The verse reflects on the far-reaching effects of neglecting family traditions, highlighting that the consequences extend beyond the individual to their descendants, leading them into a life of suffering and struggle. This notion resonates deeply within philosophical discourses about karma and dharma - the moral laws governing individual actions and their consequences. When individuals choose to prioritize personal desires over collective responsibilities, they create an imbalance that reverberates through their lineage. The unwanted population mentioned in the verse symbolizes the chaos that ensues when spiritual values are forsaken. Children born into such an environment may struggle with identity and purpose, mirroring the disarray that plagues their families.

It also urges us to reflect on the consequences of our choices, not just for ourselves but for the generations that follow. In a world increasingly driven by individualism and material pursuits, the teachings of the Geeta remind us of the importance of communal values and shared responsibilities. The act of honoring our ancestors through rituals and offerings becomes a form of spiritual nourishment, ensuring that the legacy of wisdom, love, and sacrifice continues to flow through our veins.

This highlights the consequences faced by those who neglect their familial duties. The term "hellish life" refers not just to spiritual damnation but also to the very real struggles and tribulations that arise when we forsake our roots. The offerings made to our ancestors are more than just rituals; they are essential for maintaining the harmony of our lineage.

In contemporary society, many view these practices as superstitious or unnecessary. However, this perspective often stems from a lack of understanding of their deeper significance. Rituals provide a sense of community, continuity, and purpose. They remind us of who we are, where we come from, and the responsibilities we hold toward our generations.

It is also worth noting that while the younger generations may be struggling with various issues, this does not necessarily indicate a failure on the part of their parents or ancestors. Instead, it often reflects the broader societal changes that prioritize individualism over communal values. The disconnect from ancestral practices may leave individuals feeling isolated and lost as they direct a world that values progress over tradition.

In conclusion, the importance of ancestral offerings rises above mere tradition; it is a vital practice that influences our present and future. As we embrace modernity, it is crucial not to discard the rich blend of our culture. These rituals, rooted in love, gratitude, and respect, serve as a lifeline connecting us to our past and guiding us toward a brighter future. Whether we choose to believe in the supernatural or not, the effects of our ancestors' blessings - or lack thereof - are undeniably felt in our daily lives. It is our responsibility to honor them, ensuring that their legacy continues to enrich our existence and those of generations to come.

KARMA

Q11. How does karma result?

Rather than answering the question directly, it is essential first to define what karma itself encompasses. According to ancient scriptures, every action - whether it is as subtle as breathing, blinking your eyes, or thinking, or as significant as forgiving someone or engaging in a conflict - counts as karma. In the teachings of Hindu philosophy, karma is categorized into three distinct types, each illuminating the intricate interplay between our actions and their consequences.

Sanchita Karma is like a treasure chest - or perhaps a Pandora's box - of all the deeds we've carried out across countless lifetimes. It holds every choice we've ever made, whether noble or harmful, shaping the unseen forces that guide our lives today. This stockpile of karma acts as a silent architect, influencing the joys we celebrate and the struggles we endure, as it waits patiently for the right moment to unfold.

Prarabdha Karma is like the part of your karmic story that's already in motion, influencing what you're living through right now. It's the baggage of past actions from previous lifetimes that has unfolded at the right moment into your present experiences. These aren't just random events; they're the lessons life hands you, inviting you to accept, adapt, and embrace the challenges and blessings that shape your journey today.

Kriyaman Karma, also called Agami Karma, is the karma we're creating in the present moment through our choices, actions, and intentions. It's the here and now - the decisions we make today that will shape our future. This type of karma is a reminder that we hold the power to influence what comes next, not just for ourselves but for others around us. It highlights how deeply interconnected we are, urging us to approach life with care, kindness, and mindfulness as we navigate its ups and downs.

कर्मण: सुकृतस्याहुः सात्त्विकं निर्मल फलम्।

रजसस्तु फल दुःखमज्ञानं तमसः फलम्॥ 14.16

{The result of pious action is pure and is said to be the mode of goodness. But action done in the mode of passion results in misery, and action performed in the mode of ignorance results in foolishness.}

The Bhagavad Geeta captures the essence of karma in a way that speaks straight to the soul, urging us to think deeply about our actions and their impact. It reminds us that everything we do - whether guided by kindness, ambition, or confusion - sets the tone for the life we experience. Each action carries its own energy, shaping not just the present moment but also the road we're walking toward our future.

Actions rooted in *goodness (sattvik)* come from a place of purity, kindness, and a genuine desire to uplift not just self but others. These selfless acts plant seeds of positive karma that grow and flourish over time, touching lives in ways we may never fully see. Picture a dedicated teacher who pours their heart into guiding and inspiring children - not for recognition, but out of a deep love for their duty as a teacher. The impact of their devotion goes far beyond the classroom. It lives on in the achievements of those children and the thriving, compassionate communities they help create, proving that goodness truly has a lasting influence across generations.

Lord Krishn stands as a timeless example of living with love and wisdom in every action. His teachings continue to inspire generations, showing us the transformative power of righteousness. Krishn's life is a testament to how actions done with pure intentions can lead to freedom and spiritual growth, helping the soul evolve. However, Krishn's life also encompasses many complex aspects, such as his playful side (his leelas), his strategic actions, and his involvement in battles, which may seem contradictory to the idea of pure intention. But overall, his teachings encourage aligning one's actions with higher principles, without selfish desires, to ultimately achieve liberation (moksha).

The Story of the Compassionate Farmer

In a small village, there lived a humble farmer named Chandrakant. He was known throughout the village for his kindness and generosity. Every season, he would give a portion of his harvest to the needy, even though he didn't have much to spare himself. Whether it was a hungry family or a sick elder, Chandrakant always found a way to help. He never expected anything in return - his actions were driven by a deep sense of compassion and duty.

One year, a terrible drought struck the village, leaving crops barren and many families struggling to survive. As the situation grew more dire, Chandrakant saw the suffering around him. He gathered what little he had left - some seeds and the last of his grain - and shared it with his neighbors, ensuring everyone had enough to get through the hardship.

Months later, the rains returned, and the village flourished once again. But it was Chandrakant who was rewarded in ways beyond measure. His land, which had been neglected in favor of helping others, yielded a bumper crop, the best harvest he'd ever seen. Not only did his own prosperity return, but the whole village rallied around him, repaying his kindness with their support. His selfless acts of goodness had created a ripple of goodwill that returned to him tenfold.

Chandrakant's story became a cherished legend, not just because of his good fortune, but because it showed the power of karma in the mode of goodness. By acting from a place of love and compassion, he created a legacy of kindness that benefited not only himself but the entire community. His life was a reminder that actions born from selflessness, integrity, and a genuine desire to help others are the seeds that lead to lasting rewards.

*

The results of actions performed in goodness are blessed by Mother Nature herself. On the other hand, actions driven by *passion (rajasik)* are often fueled by desires and ambitions that focus solely on personal gain. At first, these actions can seem productive, even successful. But, in reality, they often lead to inner turmoil and suffering. Take a driven entrepreneur, for example, who pushes forward in the race for success, only to sacrifice relationships and ethical values along the way. The short-term wins might look good, but eventually, the stress, dissatisfaction, and fractured connections reveal the true cost of chasing success at any price.

The Bhagavad Geeta articulates this when it describes actions done in the mode of passion: they are often accompanied by desire and an insatiable thirst for power or pleasure. Such actions may lead to temporary gains but ultimately result in disappointment and sorrow. In the Geeta's wisdom, this mode serves as a cautionary tale - reminding us that unbridled passion can entrap the soul in a cycle of suffering.

The Tale of the Greedy Merchant

Once, there was a merchant who was always on the lookout for ways to increase his wealth. Driven by ambition and the desire for more, he constantly expanded his business, acquiring as much as he could. His success seemed limitless, but his desire for profit never seemed to be satisfied. He would manipulate prices, cheat customers, and cut corners in every possible way to maximize his earnings. One day, a wise elder approached him and said, "You're chasing endless wealth, but do you ever wonder what you're sacrificing along the way?"

The merchant, blinded by greed, brushed off the elder's words and continued on his path. The more he accumulated, the more restless he became, consumed by the thought of increasing his fortune. But, as the years passed, his actions began to catch up with him. Slowly, his relationships with his family, friends, and community began to break down. People stopped trusting him. His business, once thriving, started to falter as more and more people became aware of his dishonesty.

In the end, the merchant found himself alone, surrounded by wealth but no one to share it with. His heart ached with regret, realizing too late that his relentless pursuit of wealth, driven by passion and greed, had cost him everything of true value. His karmic journey, shaped by selfish desires, had led him to ruin, showing how actions rooted in the mode of passion often bring more pain than reward.

Finally, actions performed in the mode of *ignorance (tamasik)* lead to foolishness, often causing individuals to stray from the path of righteousness. These actions stem from confusion, delusion, or a lack of understanding. Picture someone who harms others without awareness of the consequences or who clings to outdated beliefs, refusing to grow. Such actions create negative karma, fostering cycles of ignorance that are challenging to break.

In a mythological context, the story of Duryodhana from the Mahabharata comes to mind. Duryodhana, the eldest Kaurava, is a figure of ignorance and stubbornness. His refusal to acknowledge the rights of the Pandavas and his delusion of invincibility led to devastating consequences for himself and his entire kingdom. Despite possessing great power, his lack of wisdom resulted in folly, illustrating the perils of actions taken without awareness or understanding. Duryodhana's decisions, driven by jealousy and ignorance, culminated in a great war that claimed countless lives and ultimately led to his downfall (death).

*

The Tale of the Stubborn Farmer

Once, there was a farmer named Arvind, who was proud of his ability to grow crops. He had inherited a small plot of land from his father and had been working it for many years. Arvind believed that his experience alone made him the best farmer in the village. He often dismissed the advice of others, thinking that he knew better because he had been farming for so long.

One year, the weather was unpredictable. There was little rainfall, and the soil started to dry up. Many of Arvind's neighbors, who were also farmers, were worried. They listened to the weather reports and began to adjust their farming methods to conserve water. Some planted drought-resistant crops, while others built small irrigation systems to help their crops survive.

But Arvind didn't think there was any need for these precautions. He scoffed at the advice of his fellow farmers, dismissing it as unnecessary and overly cautious. "I've been farming for years," he told himself, "I've never had a problem like this before, and I won't start worrying now." Instead of taking action to adjust his methods, Arvind continued to water his crops the same way, using more water than needed, and refused to diversify his crops.

As the weeks passed, the situation worsened. Arvind's crops withered, and the water he used to irrigate them soon ran out. His fields turned brown, and he faced a severe loss. Meanwhile, his neighbors who had adapted to the conditions managed to save their crops and, in some cases, even thrived.

When the harvest came, Arvind had almost nothing to show for his efforts. He was forced to sell some of his land to make ends meet, while his neighbors flourished. He realized, too late, that his refusal to listen to others and adapt to changing circumstances had led to his downfall. His pride had clouded his judgment, and his ignorance of the new reality had cost him dearly.

Arvind's story spread through the village, and people began to talk about how his stubbornness had caused his suffering. In time, Arvind learned a valuable lesson: no matter how much experience you have, there is always room for learning and growth. Ignoring advice and refusing to adapt can lead to missed opportunities and unnecessary struggles.

From then on, Arvind became more open to learning from others, acknowledging that wisdom often comes from the experiences of others, and that being humble and adaptable can make all the difference in difficult times.

The way these different aspects of karma are connected shows how everything in life is interwoven. Every thought, choice, and action we make creates echoes that affect more than just the present moment. The consequences of what we do don't stop with us; they spread out, shaping our future and influencing the lives of those around us.

The Bhagavad Geeta encourages us to recognize that our actions, influenced by these three modes, create a cycle that is perpetuated through our choices. Understanding the nature of our actions helps us align ourselves with the path of righteousness. By recognizing the qualities of the mode of actions, we can create a legacy of love, compassion, and positivity, while acknowledging the pitfalls of passion and ignorance guides us toward personal growth and wisdom.

At its core, this question calls us to pause and really think about the impact of our actions and how they echo through the world. The Bhagavad Geeta reminds us that every choice, no matter how small, is part of the bigger story of our lives, influencing not only our own journey but also the lives of those around us. As we move forward, life constantly offers us chances to act with purpose and awareness, allowing us to be intentional in how we shape our world and the worlds of others.

यस्य सर्वे समारम्भा: कामसङ्कल्पवर्जिता: |
ज्ञानाग्निदग्धकर्माणं तमाहु: पण्डितं बुधा: || 4.19

{The enlightened sages call those persons wise, whose every action is free from the desire for material pleasures and who have burnt the reactions of work in the fire of divine knowledge.}

The verse serves as a poignant reminder to examine our motivations and the underlying energies that drive our actions. In this complex flow of karma, we're encouraged to think about what it truly means to live a life rooted in compassion, wisdom, and integrity.

As we reflect on the way our choices shape our lives, may we find the strength to act in ways that align with our truest selves. We have to remember that the legacy we create doesn't just affect our own future - it extends through time, touching others and contributing to the shared journey of humanity. Understanding karma isn't just about seeking answers; it's about embracing the power of our actions, recognizing that each step we take can transform not just our own lives, but the world around us.

Q12. Why did I suffer when I remember not performing any action (karma) related to this aspect of my life?

Lately, Shefali had become trapped in a thought that seemed both inescapable and suffocating: despite being kind, caring, and loving toward everyone around her, she still failed to receive the love she deeply longed for. It didn't seem fair. She had convinced herself that this must be the result of her karma, she couldn't recall performing. Yet, every time she looked back on her life, she saw no trace of an offense that could warrant such a lack of companionship. She had never intentionally hurt a couple, broken anyone's heart, or mistreated any man who had once liked her. The situation left her perplexed and frustrated as if the universe was punishing her for a crime she didn't remember committing. (The story of Shefali continues in question 18.)

Her internal struggle is not uncommon, and her confusion mirrors an age-old question: *Why do we suffer for actions we don't remember performing?* The answer, though simple on the surface, rests on the complex philosophy of karma - a web of past, present, and future actions that sometimes hides the cause behind the curtain of time. There are events in life that seem unwarranted, as though fate has handed us punishment for no reason. But such confusion can be untangled by looking at the following instances from the scriptures.

Echoes of Karma: Rantidev's Journey

In the ancient land of Bharata, there lived a king named Rantidev. Renowned for his unparalleled devotion, selflessness, and hospitality, he ruled with the deepest sense of compassion. His kingdom flourished, yet despite his wealth and power, he faced unimaginable trials. Throughout his life, he experienced every form of suffering one could imagine - starvation, disease, and the loss of everything he held dear. Yet, in the midst of these relentless hardships, he never wavered in his faith or kindness.

One day, as he sat in the midst of utter deprivation - his body weakened, his family gone, and his kingdom in ruins - Rantidev was approached by a series of four individuals: a Brahmana, a dog, a Chandala (a person of lower caste), and a hunter. Each of them asked for a portion of his meager food, and with each request, Rantidev, despite his own extreme hunger and suffering, shared what little he had with him. In doing so, he remained unwavering in his commitment to his dharma - to give without expecting anything in return, to act from a place of pure generosity and love.

When Rantidev finally collapsed from hunger and exhaustion, overwhelmed by the weight of his suffering, his soul called out to the Supreme Lord, Vishnu, asking, "Why, God, do I suffer like this? I have done nothing but give to others, live selflessly, and remain devoted to you. What have I done to deserve this?"

At that moment, Lord Vishnu appeared before him, surrounded by a soft, radiant light that seemed to fill the entire space. His calm yet powerful presence, and the warmth of his glow felt almost like a reassuring embrace, bringing with it a sense of peace and divine grace. With compassion, Vishnu explained to Rantidev that his suffering was not a consequence of actions he had committed in this life, but rather, it was the result of karmic debt accumulated over many lifetimes. The pain Rantidev endured was not something he deserved as punishment, but rather a spiritual test, an opportunity for him to cleanse his soul and further his path toward liberation.

"Rantidev," said Lord Vishnu!, "Your heart is pure, and your actions have been noble. But know this: every soul carries the consequences of its past actions, sometimes from lifetimes long past. What you experience now is the result of those past deeds, not of the kindness and righteousness you have shown in this life. You may not remember your past lives, nor the actions you took then, but they have a role in the unfolding of your current existence. This is the nature of karma."

Vishnu's words were a profound revelation. Though Rantidev had no memory of his past lives, his suffering was part of a larger karmic cycle, beyond his control. Yet, Lord Vishnu reassured him that through his steadfast devotion and actions, he was cleansing those very debts. True spiritual growth comes not from avoiding suffering, but from embracing it with grace, understanding, and the wisdom to see beyond the pain to the lessons it brings.

After hearing these divine words, Rantidev found peace. His suffering, which had once seemed endless and unjust, now made sense to him. He understood that every action, every choice, every thought - whether in this life or previous ones - had a flowing effect on his journey. But rather than succumbing to bitterness or despair, Rantidev chose to remain faithful, to endure with patience, knowing that his soul was being purified through each hardship.

And as Lord Vishnu smiled upon him, Rantidev's heart swelled with a deep sense of gratitude, not for the end of his suffering, but for the wisdom and insight he had gained from it.

*

From Thorns to Arrows: Bhishma's Unfolding Fate

In the battle of Kurukshetra, Bhishma was critically wounded by Arjun's arrows but was not killed because of his boon of Ichha Mrityu (the ability to choose the time of his death). Bhishma, who was lying on the bed of arrows, saw the sun about to set, and he called Krishn to his side. With great reverence, he addressed him, saying:

> "O Krishn, I have been pierced by Arjun's arrows, and I shall not leave my body until I have imparted all that I have learned about dharma and the soul." (Shanti Parva 9.48)

> "Bhishma asked Krishn, 'O Krishn, how does the soul depart from the body? What happens to the soul after death? Please explain this to me, as I am about to leave this body." (Shanti Parva 9.50)

> "O Bhishma, it is through the law of karma that individuals experience the fruits of their past actions. Even though

> you are a person of great virtue, your present suffering is the result of the karma from your past births. Just as a person must experience the consequences of actions from a previous life, so must you bear the results of your past karma, which is why you are here, on this bed of arrows." (Shanti Parva 9.51)

Krishn explains that the results of one's past actions, even from previous lifetimes, are never completely erased and can manifest at any time based on the nature of the accumulated karma.

Krishn goes on to explain that the wheel of karma is very intricate, and while some may suffer due to past misdeeds, others may be blessed due to their good actions in past lives. Bhishma's predicament, in this case, is not due to any fault in his present life but is the result of actions from earlier lifetimes.

> "Krishn replied, 'The soul is eternal, it does not perish when the body perishes. Just as a person discards old clothes and puts on new ones, similarly, the soul discards the old body and enters a new one." (Shanti Parva 9.52)

> "Bhishma said, 'O Krishn, I have always followed dharma, even when it was difficult. I performed my duties without attachment to the results, and my actions were done with sincerity. However, I am aware that the consequences of my past actions have led me to this fate. But I am at peace, for I know that I will attain liberation through my understanding of dharma." (Shanti Parva 9.61)

Krishn goes on to explain that the wheel of karma is very intricate, and while some may suffer due to past misdeeds, others may be blessed due to their good actions in past lives. Bhishma's predicament, in this case, is not due to any fault in his present life but is the result of actions from earlier lifetimes.

> "The soul is subject to the consequences of its past actions, and those actions are the root cause of both pleasure and pain in this life and the next." (Shanti Parva 184.41)

As found in some secondary interpretations and through

various commentaries and regional mythologies, Bhishma's story provides us with deep insight into the workings of karma. At the end of the great war of Kurukshetra, when Krishn finally stood before him, Bhishma - despite his agony - greeted the divine lord with praises and humility. But amidst the reverence, Bhishma asked Krishn a question that had been troubling his soul as Bhishma had a divine sense to go back to his past lives till 100 births: "Why am I suffering this way, despite having walked the path of dharma throughout my life? Why must I endure such a cruel fate when I have lived righteously?"

Krishn's response was as profound as it was revealing. He reminded Bhishma that while he had not committed any sin in his recent lifetimes - spanning over one hundred births - there was an unresolved karma from his one hundred and first birth. During that lifetime, Bhishma, then in a different form, had thrown a snake in thorns, inflicting pain on him. That act had remained dormant in his karmic reservoir for lifetimes, as Bhishma had lived virtuously since. However, now that he had allied himself with Duryodhana, who represented adharma (unrighteousness), the long-forgotten karma resurfaced. The thorns once experienced by the snake because of him now appeared as the arrows impaling his body, forcing him to endure the consequences of that distant action.

*

This story beautifully encapsulates a core principle of karma: *our actions, even the smallest ones, are never truly lost - they follow us, quietly waiting for the right moment to bear fruit.* Whether good or bad, the results of karma do not always manifest immediately. Just as seeds sown in a field take time to sprout and grow, karma, too, follows a timeline beyond our comprehension. Some actions ripen quickly, while others may take lifetimes to manifest.

न हि कश्चित्क्षणमपि जातु तिष्ठत्यकर्मकृत्।
कार्यते ह्यवशः कर्म सर्वः प्रकृतिजैर्गुणैः ॥ 3.5

{Everyone is forced to act helplessly according to the qualities he has acquired from the modes of material nature; therefore no one can refrain from doing something, not even for a moment.}

Even when we believe we are not acting, we are always engaged in some form of karma - whether it be physical actions, thoughts, or intentions. Some karmas are performed so unconsciously or in such minor ways that we don't even remember them. Yet, these seemingly insignificant actions accumulate over time, just like drops of water filling a jar.

In Shefali's case, the suffering she experiences may not be the result of any action she performed in her current life but could very well stem from Prarabdha Karma - the collection of accumulated deeds from all her past lives. According to Hindu philosophy, every soul carries forward a reservoir of past actions, both virtuous and sinful, which shape the experiences of future lifetimes. Some karmas lie dormant, waiting for the right circumstances to unfold, much like Bhishma's thorn-inflicted karma.

बहूनि मे व्यतीतानि जन्मानि तव चार्जुन।
तान्यहं वेद सर्वाणि न त्वं वेत्थ परन्तप॥ 4.5

{The Personality of Godhead said: Many, many births both you and I have passed. I can remember all of them, but you cannot, O subduer of the enemy!}

Ordinary humans are unable to recall the actions performed in previous incarnations, unlike Bhishma. The karmas we carry are often hidden from us, buried deep within the unconscious realms of the soul. This can lead to moments of bewilderment, as Shefali experiences where we are forced to face consequences without understanding their origin.

The concept of Prarabdha Karma - the portion of karma

that is ripe and ready to bear fruit in this lifetime offers another layer of insight. Not all of our accumulated actions will affect us at once; only those karmas that have matured influence the present. Shefali's heartbreak could be the manifestation of such a karma - something she set into motion lifetimes ago, now coming to fruition. Just as Bhishma's suffering arose when he aligned with adharma, Shefali's experiences may have been triggered by subtle actions from her past or associations that unknowingly shaped her current reality.

This idea leads to an essential truth: *karma operates beyond the boundaries of logic and memory*. It doesn't adhere to a linear timeline or a cause-and-effect system that we can easily trace. Instead, karma unfolds like a cosmic dance, with each step revealing itself only when the time is right.

So, why does Shefali suffer despite having no recollection of performing harmful actions? The answer lies in the deep, intricate nature of karma. Just as seeds planted in darkness grow unseen until they sprout, the consequences of our past actions - whether from this life or many lifetimes ago - can emerge unexpectedly. This is not a punishment but a reminder that every action leaves an imprint, no matter how distant or forgotten. It urges us to embrace humility and surrender, knowing that the results of our karma are beyond our immediate understanding.

Shefali's longing for love and the emptiness she felt are not necessarily the result of deliberate wrongdoing. They could be lessons her soul needs to experience for reasons known only to the universe. Karma isn't always about retribution - it's also about growth, learning, and the soul's journey toward self-realization (question 21). Sometimes, suffering comes in the form of a teacher, guiding us toward deeper wisdom and compassion.

The Geeta offers solace in this regard. It reminds us that the soul is eternal and ever-evolving, moving through countless lifetimes in pursuit of truth and liberation. While we may not always comprehend the reasons behind our suffering, we are urged to trust in the process and continue walking the path of dharma with faith and patience.

In Shefali's example, the answer to her question may not lie in dissecting her past actions or searching for mistakes but in accepting the unfolding of karma with grace. Her experiences, though painful, are part of a larger landscape - a journey her soul must undertake to grow and evolve. Just as Bhishma found peace on his bed of arrows by surrendering to Krishn's divine will, Shefali, too, might find solace by trusting that the love she seeks will come in its own time, when her karma aligns with her deep-seated wish.

In the grand scheme of things, karma is not merely about reward and punishment - it is a force that shapes our spiritual evolution. Every experience, whether joyous or painful, serves a purpose in the journey toward self-discovery and inner peace. And while we may not always remember the actions that led to our current reality, the

Geeta teaches us to act with awareness and kindness, knowing that each moment carries the potential to transform our destiny.

Thus, the question is not simply about why Shefali suffers but rather about how she chooses to respond to that suffering. *The fruits of karma may be inevitable, but the way we cultivate our inner garden through acceptance, surrender, and love shapes the beauty that blooms from it.*

Q13. How do I attain peace from unknown or unintentional karma?

In life, we sometimes find ourselves burdened by unexplained suffering, as if fate has dealt us a hand we don't deserve. These moments feel especially unfair because we can't recall any wrongdoing that might have caused our current difficulties. The idea of unknown or unintentional karma - the fruits of actions we performed in previous lives or even in this one without conscious intent - can seem overwhelming. The Bhagavad Geeta offers a path to peace, for when faced with such invisible burdens.

युक्तः कर्मफलं त्यक्त्वा शान्तिमाप्नोति नैष्ठिकीम् ।
अयुक्तः कामकारेण फले सक्तो निबध्यते ॥ 5.12

{The steadily devoted soul attains unadulterated peace because he offers the result of all activities to Me. A person who is attached to the fruits of their labor becomes entangled.}

The moment we learn that karma governs our lives, a sense of fear often creeps in. We wonder how many invisible karmic debts we carry and whether unpleasant outcomes await us. Even if we project joy on the surface, there is often a quiet restlessness within. Fear of the unknown - of the karmic seeds we never realized we sowed. But, as Krishn teaches, peace lies not in unraveling the past but in surrendering to the divine in the present.

One of the greatest challenges with karma is that we cannot consciously perceive every action's effect. Some karmic outcomes arise from deeds in previous lifetimes - completely beyond our knowledge. Trying to consciously fix these unknown debts can feel like chasing shadows. However, we are reassured that it is possible to cleanse even hidden karma through surrender, devotion, and faith.

ब्रह्मण्याधाय कर्माणि सङ्गं त्यक्त्वा करोति यः।
लिप्यते न स पापेन पद्मपत्रमिवाम्भसा ॥ 5.10

{One who performs his duty without attachment, surrendering the results to the Supreme, is untouched by sinful action - just like a lotus leaf remains untouched by water.}

For those of us leading busy lives, the idea of uninterrupted worship may feel daunting. But peace through surrender does not demand grand gestures. Krishn suggests in Geeta to start small - by offering our daily actions to Him. The ritual is simple as follows: Take five minutes every night before going to sleep and talk to Krishn, as if speaking to a friend. Say: "*Every action I took today, I offer to Your divine feet.*"

At first, this ritual might feel awkward. We are painfully aware of the good and bad actions we perform throughout the day. Offering our shortcomings at Krishn's feet may stir discomfort. But this discomfort is not a flaw - it's a seed of transformation. As we reflect on our day, we begin to ask ourselves: If I am offering my actions to Krishn, shouldn't I act righteously? This subtle shift marks the beginning of our spiritual growth.

Gradually, this nightly surrender reshapes us from within. Over time, we become more mindful of our choices throughout the day, guided by the awareness that every action is ultimately offered to Krishn. This practice not only prevents us from creating new karmic debts but also helps dissolve the burdens of past actions, one by one.

Many people approach God with desires - hoping for material rewards, success, or relationships. But the Bhagavad Geeta teaches that such attachments keep us bound to the cycle of karma. True peace comes when we worship without expecting rewards, loving Krishn for who He is rather than what He can provide.

यत्करोषि यदश्नासि यज्जुहोषि ददासि यत्।
यत्तपस्यसि कौन्तेय तत्कुरुष्व मदर्पणम्॥ 9.27

{Whatever you do, whatever you eat, whatever you offer or give away, and whatever austerities you perform - do that, O son of Kunti, as an offering to Me.}

By surrendering every action, no matter how ordinary or sacred, we align with divine will. Life becomes a flowing river of trust, where we no longer worry about outcomes. With Krishn guiding us, we act with sincerity and let go of the need for control. This trust frees us from anxiety and opens the door to inner peace.

While nightly surrender offers immense relief, some karmic debts - known as prarabdha karma - must still be experienced in this lifetime. One cannot escape the suffering of prarabdha but can surely get the strength to face the outcomes. These are the fruits of actions destined to unfold, regardless of surrender. However, even these burdens become lighter when we walk the path of devotion. Krishn protects His devotees from unbearable suffering.

This doesn't mean that surrender guarantees the fulfillment of personal desires. For example, Shefali, who has dedicated her heart to Krishn, may not get her ex back or find a partner immediately. But her suffering will cease to hold power over her. With her heart anchored in Krishn's love, external circumstances lose their ability to disrupt her inner peace. She learns to trust that whatever unfolds is part of a divine plan, beyond her understanding.

शुभाशुभफलैरेवं मोक्ष्यसे कर्मबन्धनैः।
सन्न्यासयोगयुक्तात्मा विमुक्तो मामुपैष्यसि॥ 9.28

{In this way you will be freed from bondage to action and its auspicious and inauspicious results. With your mind fixed on Me in this principle of renunciation, you will be liberated and come to Me.}

Krishn's teachings invite us to live like the lotus - rooted in the mud, yet untouched by it. The lotus leaf floats above the water, never absorbing it. Similarly, when we surrender our actions and their outcomes to Krishn, we engage with life fully, yet remain unaffected by its turbulence of the material world we live in.

Ultimately, peace comes not from controlling life's outcomes but from trusting that Krishn holds us in His care. Whether joy or sorrow visits us, we remain steady, knowing that every experience serves a divine purpose.

भोक्तारं यज्ञतपसां सर्वलोकमहेश्वरम् ।
सुहृदं सर्वभूतानां ज्ञात्वा मां शान्तिमृच्छति ॥ 5.29

{A person in full consciousness of Me, knowing Me to be the ultimate beneficiary of all sacrifices and austerities, the Supreme Lord of all, and the well-wisher of all beings, attains peace from the pangs of material miseries.}

In surrendering to Krishn, we discover a peace that transcends logic and circumstance. The burdens of unknown karma no longer haunt us, for they rest in divine hands. With every act we offer to Him, our hearts grow lighter, and our souls become freer.

This journey is not about perfection - it is about trust. The peace we seek comes not from undoing the past but from living with faith in the present. In Krishn's love, we find the courage to embrace life fully, knowing that whatever karma may arise, we are held by the divine.

This surrender reveals the beauty of divine grace. Even the heaviest burdens become light when placed at Krishn's feet. The peace we discover flows not from worldly rewards or external events but from a trust that transcends all circumstances. With our hearts dedicated to Krishn, we live in alignment with divine will - content, free, and untouched by life's storms.

Q14. How does karma get carried forward from one life to another if the soul is not entangled with the material body?

The soul's journey is a symphony, composed of countless notes from past lives, harmonizing into the melody of existence. Every experience, emotion, and action plays a role in shaping this intricate design, forming the patterns of our karma. The effects of our past actions extend into the present, shaping our current reality and leading us toward what lies ahead. At the core of this understanding is an important truth: while the soul remains separate and untouched by the physical body, it still carries the marks of its past actions into each new life it enters.

यथा सर्वगतं सौक्ष्म्यादाकाशं नोपलिप्यते।
सर्वत्रावस्थितो देहे तथात्मा नोपलिप्यते॥ 13.32

{Just as the all-pervading ether does not become contaminated despite being present everywhere, the soul is not affected by its association with the body.}

This verse highlights a fundamental truth: the soul, like the ethereal space around us, remains untouched by the physical vessel it inhabits. Yet, the question arises - how does karma, a reflection of past actions, carry forward if the soul itself is not entangled in the material world?

To comprehend this phenomenon, we must first grasp the essence of the soul. The Bhagavad Geeta presents the soul as eternal, immutable, and separate from the ever-changing physical body. While the body experiences the cycles of birth, growth, decay, and death, the soul remains constant, akin to the sun that shines regardless of the clouds that momentarily obscure it.

Yet, despite its untainted nature, the soul does not exist in isolation; it is engaged in a continuous journey through the realms of existence. Each lifetime is a chapter in the soul's evolution, influenced by the choices made in previous incarnations. Karma serves as the bridge that connects these chapters, ensuring that the actions of one life reverberate through time, shaping the experiences of the next.

देहिनोऽस्मिन्यथा देहे कौमारं यौवनं जरा।
तथा देहान्तरप्राप्तिर्धीरस्तत्र न मुह्यति॥ 2.13

{Just as the body undergoes changes from childhood to old age, the soul transitions from one body to another. The wise, however, are not deluded by this.}

To further elaborate on the soul's transcendental nature and its journey through the material world, Shrimad Bhagavata Mahapurana offers deeper insights in the following verses.

प्रकृतिस्थोऽपि पुरुषो नाज्यते प्राकृतैर्गुणैः |
अविकारादकर्तृत्वान्निर्गुणत्वाज्जलार्कवत् || 1 ||
स एष यर्हि प्रकृतेर्गुणेष्वभिविषज्जते |
अहङ्क्रियाविमूढात्मा कर्तास्मीति अभिमन्यते || 2 ||
तेन संसारपदवीं अवशोऽभ्येत्यनिवृतः |
प्रासङ्गिकैः कर्मदोषैः सदसन्मिश्रयोनिṣu || 3 ||
अर्थे ह्यविद्यमानेऽपि संसृतिर्न निवर्तते |
ध्यायतः विषयानस्य स्वप्नेऽनर्थागमो यथा || 4 ||
अत एव शनैश्चित्तं प्रसक्तं असतां पथि |
भक्तियोगेन तीव्रेण विरक्त्या च नयेद्वशम् || 5 ||

{The Supreme Lord [as Kapila] said: 'Even though the living entity abides in a material body, he is not affected by the basic qualities of matter when he does not claim proprietorship and thus is not subject to change, just like the sun that is not affected by being reflected in water.

When one thus considers the modes [of goodness, passion, and ignorance] without attachment, understanding them to be the cause of the different conditions of the self, one obtains [back] the original position of transcendence [svarūpa].

The individual soul, transcendental as he is, because of his attention to the modes of nature, becomes dependent, but when he is a witness who is not attached to the modes, he is a Lord without endeavor.

When one is not attached to the modes of nature and the material body, and has no desire to enjoy, then the consciousness of the knower of the field becomes clear.

When one, by means of this transcendental knowledge, always is of service unto Me with love and devotion, one will achieve the pure existence of spiritual and supreme peace.'}

सेयं भगवतो माया यन्नयेन विरुध्यते |

ईश्वरस्य विमुक्तस्य कार्पण्यमुत बन्धनम् || 9 ||

यदर्थेन विना मूष्य पुंस आत्मविपर्ययः |

प्रतीयत उपद्रष्टुः स्वशिरश्छेदनादिकः || 10 ||

यथा जले चन्द्रमसः कम्पादिस्तत्कृतो गुणः ।
दृश्यतेऽसन्नपि द्रष्टुः आत्मनोऽनात्मनो गुणः ।। 11 ।।

{This is the illusory energy of the Supreme Lord by which the living entity, although transcendental to the modes of nature, thinks of himself as a product of material nature.

Due to this external energy, the living entity, although transcendental to the three modes of material nature, thinks of himself as a material product and thus undergoes the reactions of material miseries.

The spirit soul, bewildered by the influence of false ego, thinks himself the doer of activities that are in actuality carried out by the three modes of material nature.}

यथा पुत्राच्च वित्ताच्च पृथङ्मर्त्यः प्रतीयते।
अप्यात्मत्वेनाभिमताद्देहादेः पुरुषस्तथा॥ 39
यथोल्मुकाद्विस्फुलिङ्गाद्धूमाद्वापि स्वसंभवात्।
अप्यात्मत्वेनाभिमताद्यथाग्निः पृथगुल्मुकात्॥ 40
भूतेंद्रियान्तःकरणात्प्रधानाज्जीवसंज्ञितात्।
आत्मा तथा पृथग्द्रष्टा भगवान्ब्रह्मसंज्ञितः॥ 41

सर्वभूतेषु चात्मानं सर्वभूतानि चात्मनि।

ईक्षेतानन्यभावेन भूतेष्विव तदात्मताम्॥ 42

स्वयोनिषु यथा ज्योतिरेकं नाना प्रतीयते।

योनीनां गुणवैषम्यात्तथात्मा प्रकृतौ स्थितः॥43

तस्मादिमां स्वां प्रकृतिं दैवीं सदसदात्मिकाम्।

दुर्विभाव्यां पराभाव्य स्वरूपेणावतिष्ठते॥ 44

{The way a mortal man is understood as being different from his son and wealth, irrespective his natural inclination for them, so too a person in his original nature differs from his body, senses, mind and such [irrespective his identification with them].

It is like with a fire that differs from its flames, sparks and smoke, although they by nature, being produced by itself, are intimately associated with it. The elements, the senses, the mind and the primary nature of the individual soul, the same way differs from the seer, who is the Supreme Lord who is known as the spiritual complete [Brahman].

The way one with an equal mind sees all creatures as being part of the same natural order, one should also see the soul as being present in all manifestations and all manifestations in the soul.

Just like the one fire manifests itself in different types of wood, so too the one spiritual soul, in its position in material nature, knows different births under different natural conditions.}

एकः शुद्धः स्वयंज्योतिः निर्गुणोऽसौ गुणाश्रयः ।
सर्वगोऽनावृतः साक्षी निरात्माात्मात्मनः परः ।। 7 ।।
य एवं संतमात्मानं आत्मस्थं वेद पुरुषः ।
नाज्यते प्रकृतिस्थोऽपि तद्गुणैः स मयि स्थितः ।। 8 ।।

{In other words, which person having life experience would in his detachment call himself the proprietor of the wealth, house and children that result from such a bodily concept?

The one pure self that is enlightened and free from material characteristics, constitutes the reservoir of all good qualities that, transcendental to the body and the mind and pervading all, is the undivided witness unrelated to the material world.}

The Supreme Lord, in His incarnation as Kapila, explains the real nature of the soul and how it becomes entangled in the material world. He compares the soul to the sun, which remains unaffected even when its reflection appears in water. Similarly, even though the soul is inside a material body, it remains untouched by the qualities of material nature - as long as it does not claim ownership over anything. The moment we think, *"This is mine, I am in control,"* we start identifying with the body and material experiences, which makes us vulnerable to change and suffering.

Everything we experience - happiness, sorrow, desires, and struggles - is influenced by the three modes of nature: goodness, passion, and ignorance. These modes are like different filters through which we perceive life. If we understand that these modes, and not our true self, are responsible for our changing moods and circumstances, we can begin to rise above them. When we stop identifying with them, we regain our true, spiritual nature (svaroopa).

However, when the soul forgets its spiritual identity and starts paying attention to the material world, it becomes dependent on these modes. It loses its natural state of freedom and mistakenly believes that it is the doer of all actions. But in reality, the three modes are carrying out everything. The soul is simply witnessing. If we remain detached, without trying to control or claim things as ours, we become free - just like a king who rules effortlessly rather than being controlled by external forces.

The key to achieving this clarity is letting go of attachment to the material body and its pleasures. When a person sees life without selfish desires and understands the deeper truth, their consciousness becomes purified. They begin to see things as they really are. This realization allows one to serve the Supreme Lord with love and devotion, which leads to a state of true peace and spiritual fulfillment.

But what keeps us trapped in illusion? The Lord explains that it is His own illusory energy, *maya*, that makes the soul forget its transcendental nature. Though the soul is naturally beyond material nature, it starts believing that it is a part of it. Because of this illusion, we experience suffering, thinking we are the body rather than the eternal soul. The false ego - the sense of "*I am doing this, I am the controller*" - makes us believe that we are the cause of our actions. But in reality, everything happens due to the three modes of nature.

Just as one grows from infancy to old age, the soul moves through various lives, carrying with it the essence of its past actions. Those with wisdom see this truth, knowing that while the physical body may perish, the soul's journey continues. Because it is not that body that performs an action, it is the soul (mann) that encourages the body to provide satisfaction from sensory objects, since the soul cannot achieve anything by all itself – it needs a medium (body) to act.

The soul, while pure, accumulates the consequences of its actions throughout its various incarnations. These consequences, referred to as karmic imprints, shape the soul's future experiences. Every thought, word, and action generates an echo that remains woven into the essence of the soul, akin to waves on the surface of a lake.

Karma operates on the principle of cause and effect; it is a cosmic ledger where every action is recorded and evaluated. When the soul departs from one physical form, it carries with it the residual energy of its past actions, which in turn dictates the circumstances of its next life. This karmic residue is not a burden but rather a guiding force, steering the soul towards lessons it must learn in its quest for spiritual evolution.

At the heart of karma lies intention. Actions driven by pure intentions, aligned with dharma (righteousness), yield positive karma. Conversely, actions rooted in selfish desires and ignorance may produce negative consequences. Thus, the quality of one's intentions significantly influences the karmic outcomes that follow.

In this context, karma becomes a reflection of the soul's growth. Each lifetime offers opportunities for the soul to refine itself, learn from past mistakes, and evolve toward higher consciousness. The more the soul engages in righteous actions with selfless intentions, the more it aligns itself with divine will, enabling it to transcend the entanglements of the material world.

The process by which karma carries forward is not arbitrary; it is a manifestation of divine justice. The universe operates on the principle of balance, ensuring that every action has a corresponding consequence. Much like Newton's third law of motion, which states that *'every action has an equal and opposite reaction,'* the karmic law reflects this same truth. Just as physical actions yield predictable reactions, our thoughts, words, and deeds generate consequences that resonate through the pattern of existence, echoing back to us in ways we may not always immediately comprehend. This complex chain of cause and effect allows for growth and learning, providing the soul with the necessary experiences to evolve.

Karma serves as both a teacher and a guide, facilitating the soul's journey towards enlightenment. By experiencing the fruits of past actions, the soul gains wisdom and understanding, enabling it to make better choices in the future. This cyclical nature of karma is akin to a spiral staircase; each step taken represents a lesson learned, bringing the soul closer to liberation.

Ultimately, the goal of understanding karma and its workings is to achieve liberation (*moksha*). The Bhagavad Geeta reveals that by realizing the true nature of the self and surrendering to the divine, the soul can transcend the cycle of birth, death and rebirth. When one acts without attachment to the results, dedicating every action to the Supreme, the binding effects of karma diminish.

It can be revealed that there is profound interconnectedness between our actions and their consequences. The soul, though eternal and pure, carries the marks of the choices it makes, shaping its path through the cycles of rebirth. When we understand this connection, we can live more mindfully and with greater purpose.

Hence karma is carried forward from one life to another through the subtle, immaterial aspects of the soul. While the body is temporary and changes with each rebirth, the soul remains constant, carrying with it the impressions of past actions. These impressions, or *samskaras*, form the underlying patterns that influence the soul's choices and experiences in future lives. Even though the soul is not directly entangled with the material body, its journey through different lives is shaped by the accumulated karma, which guides the soul toward lessons and growth. In this way, karma is not bound by the physical form but remains a thread connecting one lifetime to the next, influencing the soul's evolution.

MEDITATION

Q15. How to meditate?

An expression of failure pops up as soon as we hear the word "meditation". It is an instantaneous response from our brain to this particular word. During conversations about meditation with friends or spiritual guides, the term transforms into a daunting challenge, appearing as complex as rocket science. We have delusionally convinced ourselves that mastering it is beyond our reach due to the intricate processes we've unconsciously assigned to it. However, the truth is that meditation is a remarkably simple practice that can seamlessly enhance our daily lives and contribute to our overall well-being.

An ancient story tells of how a concept of meditation emerged when even the most dedicated sages struggled to maintain their focus. In their quest for clarity and enlightenment, they discovered a method that would become foundational. They used the flame of a lamp as a focal point, directing their attention toward this simple object. The essence of this practice lay in their difficulty concentrating their minds at a single point, particularly between the eyebrows. It is indeed challenging to center our thoughts without letting them drift in various directions, leading to inevitable distractions. Even these exalted beings, powerful and detached from worldly attachments, found it daunting to keep their minds anchored. For ordinary individuals like us, having a tangible focal point becomes essential in the meditative journey.

Given our faith in spirituality, establishing a meaningful relationship with the Supreme is crucial for attaining the highest states of meditation. This journey requires us to cultivate self-awareness regarding our physical and mental states, understanding our desires and the potential outcomes.

In the *Shrimad Bhagavad Geeta*, Lord Krishn provides guidance on meditation, presenting a simple and effective approach. The first step involves finding a secluded spot where one can sit in solitude, letting go of all desires associated with the process while striving to gain control over the mind. Although achieving a state devoid of thoughts may seem impossible, this should not discourage us. Krishn's teachings illuminate the path through comprehensible English translations of the sacred verses as follows.

योगी युञ्जीत सत्त्वात्मानं रहसि स्थितः।
एकाकी यतचित्तात्मा निराशीरपरिग्रहः ॥ 6.10

{A transcendentalist should always engage his body, mind, and self in relationship with the Supreme; he should live alone in a secluded place and always carefully control his mind. He should be free from desires and feelings of possessiveness.}

शुचौ देशे प्रतिष्ठाप्य स्थिरमासनमात्मनः।
नात्युच्छ्रितं नातिनीचं चैलाजिनकुशोत्तरम्॥ 6.11

{To practice yoga, one should go to a secluded place and lay kusha grass on the ground, covering it with a deerskin and a soft cloth. The seat should be neither too high nor too low and situated in a sacred place.}

तत्रैकाग्रं मनः कृत्वा यतचित्तेन्द्रियक्रियः।
उपविश्यासनं युञ्जीयाद्योगमात्मविशुद्धये॥ 6.12

{There, with a focused mind, one should practice yoga for the purification of the self.}

समं कायशिरोग्रीवं धारयन्नचलं स्थिरः।
सम्प्रेक्ष्य नासिकाग्रं स्वदिशश्चानवलोकयन्॥ 6.13

{One should hold one's body, neck, and head erect in a straight line and stare steadily at the tip of the nose.}

प्रशान्तात्मा विगतभीर्ब्रह्मचारिव्रते स्थितः।
मनः संयम्य मच्चित्तो युक्त आसीत मत्परः॥ 6.14

{Thus, with an unagitated, subdued mind, devoid of fear, completely free from sex life, one should meditate upon Me with the heart and make Me the ultimate goal of life.}

युञ्जन्नेवं सदा आत्मानं योगी नियतमानसः।
शान्तिं निर्वाणपरमां मत्संस्थामधिगच्छति॥ 6.15

{Thus practicing constant control of the body, mind, and activities, the mystic transcendentalist, his mind regulated, attains the kingdom of God by cessation of material existence.}

सङ्कल्पप्रभवान्कामांस्त्यक्त्वा सर्वानशेषतः।
मनसैवेन्द्रियग्रामं विनियम्य समन्ततः ॥ 6.24

{One should engage oneself in the practice of yoga with determination and faith and not be deviated from the path. One should abandon, without exception, all material desires born of mental speculation and control all the senses on all sides by the mind.}

शनैः शनैरुपरमेदबुद्ध्या धृतिगृहीतया।
आत्मसंस्थं मनः कृत्वा न किञ्चिदपि चिन्तयेत् ॥ 6.25

{Gradually, step by step, one should become situated in trance by means of intelligence sustained by full conviction, and thus the mind should be fixed on the self alone and should think of nothing else.}

यतो यतो निश्चरति मनश्चञ्चलमस्थिरम्।
ततस्ततो नियम्यैतदात्मन्येव वशं नयेत्॥ 6.26

{From wherever the mind wanders due to its flickering and unsteady nature, one must certainly withdraw it and bring it back under the control of the self.}

Recognizing that it can be difficult to maintain focus without an external medium, one can sit comfortably, close their eyes, and visualize the divine image of God. Allow your mind to immerse itself in the grace of the Supreme while dismissing the distractions of material life. Become absorbed in the beauty of His lotus feet, the enchanting sound of His melodious flute, the sweet smile that could charm even the most skeptical, and the depths of His ocean-like eyes.

Yet, our restless minds often divert our attention, particularly in a world fixated on material gain. Our thoughts can remain restless even during sleep, stubbornly focused on desires that demand fulfillment. To address this, God offers sage advice, urging us to practice diligently. Regardless of how often our thoughts stray, we must gently guide them back to our focal point and continue our practice.

चञ्चलं हि मनः कृष्ण प्रमाथि बलवद्दृढम्।
तस्याहं निग्रहं मन्ये वायोरिव सुदुष्करम्॥ 6.34

{For the mind is restless, turbulent, obstinate, and very strong, O Krishn, and to subdue it, I think, is more difficult than controlling the wind.}

असंशयं महाबाहो मनो दुर्निग्रहं चलम्।
अभ्यासेन तु कौन्तेय वैराग्येण च गृह्यते॥ 6.35

{O mighty-armed son of Kunti, it is undoubtedly very difficult to curb the restless mind, but it is possible by suitable practice and by detachment.}

This method resonates most profoundly with those who are faithful in Krishn. It is likely that devotees of Krishn can readily envision His divine beauty and become absorbed in His form. However, even those who do not subscribe to a belief in God can begin their meditation journey by focusing on their breath - the incoming and outgoing flow. The key lies in simply observing this rhythm, which can evoke a sense of tranquility and relief. I learnt this method in my Vipassana meditation retreat which is truly soothing in itself and has its own magic.

Yet another, meditation technique, which I learned during my Reiki practice, has become a cherished part of my spiritual journey. While many guided meditations abound online, this one speaks to me deeply, like a song that lingers long after the last note fades. I feel compelled to share it, hoping it will inspire others as it has inspired me. I express my heartfelt gratitude to my Reiki master, Mr. Ajit Telave - a soul full of quiet magic and profound wisdom.

Begin by finding a quiet, sacred space - whether it's the floor, a chair, or your bed. Settle comfortably and close your eyes. With a long, steady breath, release the weight of the world from your shoulders. Now, visualize a radiant golden ball, spinning gently on its axis, about two inches across and glowing six inches above your head. This sphere is the symbol of your pure consciousness - shining, steady, infinite. Slowly, it descends toward your *Sahasrara* (crown) chakra, an ocean of deep violet swirling just above your head. As the golden ball melts into the violet pool, imagine streams of light radiating outward - sometimes golden, sometimes violet, and other times a perfect blend of both. These luminous rays dance around you like waves of energy, extending beyond your body and weaving a silent connection between your soul and the boundless divine. You are now the center of this radiant wheel, and the universe recognizes the quiet harmony within you.

The ball drifts lower, drawn toward the *Ajna* (third eye) chakra nestled between your brows, a deep blue gateway to higher perception and inner knowing. As the ball merges with this indigo realm, cascades of gold and blue light ripple outward, gently spinning in all directions. In this moment, clarity emerges. Your life's purpose stirs, like petals unfolding at dawn, and the world bears witness to your awakening, recognizing the profound truths beginning to bloom within you.

The ball now glides gracefully toward the *Vishuddha* (throat) chakra, shimmering in soft blue - the sacred space where wisdom, learning, and expression reside. As the golden ball sinks into the cool light of this chakra, rays of golden-blue hues spiral outward like a whisper carried by the wind. The energy of transformation surrounds you, shifting sorrow into serenity, confusion into clarity. Your every experience is now a thread in the grand canvas of becoming. The universe feels your renewal, and the light within you grows stronger.

Slowly, the ball drifts into the *Anahata* (heart) chakra, glowing with vibrant green - the seat of unconditional love and compassion. It merges completely with this emerald radiance, releasing waves of golden-green light that flow in every direction like a warm embrace. You feel love radiating from your being - boundless, pure, unburdened by expectations. Picture someone you cherish, and let the memory bloom within your heart. The love surrounding you deepens, filling the air with tenderness, as though every heartbeat carries a message of affection to the world.

The ball descends further, toward the *Manipura* (solar plexus) chakra - a bright yellow center of courage, wisdom, and power. As it sinks into the golden-yellow light, the energy around you swells, radiating strength and confidence. Feel this power coursing through you - steady and unwavering, like the sun at midday. The world acknowledges your inner fire, the quiet brilliance that guides you through life's challenges. In this moment, you know the truth of your own strength, and it lights the path before you.

The ball continues downward into the *Swadhisthana* (sacral) chakra, a vivid orange center of joy and creativity. Here, the golden sphere dissolves fully into the chakra, releasing glowing rays of orange-gold light that spread outward like the hues of a sunset. Breathe deeply, and feel peace settling over you - a serenity as still as twilight. In this space, joy flows effortlessly. Everything around you has become calm, bathed in the gentle glow of your inner contentment.

Finally, the ball descends to the *Muladhara* (root) chakra, the foundation of stability, glowing a deep, grounded red. As the golden ball merges with this base chakra, rays of red and gold intertwine, creating an aura of security and balance.

The earth beneath you responds, recognizing the strength of your roots, the steadiness of your presence. You are grounded and protected, a pillar of quiet assurance. The world sees how deeply connected you are to the rhythms of the earth, and you feel unshaken, no matter what storms may arise.

With its descent complete, the golden ball begins to rise again, moving gently upward. It pauses once more at the *Swadhisthana* chakra, the wellspring of joy and peace. Here, the golden-orange light expands outward, enveloping you and everything around you. The sunset glow lingers, as if time itself has stilled. In this moment, there is nothing but peace - absolute, undisturbed. All suffering has dissolved, and no sorrow touches you. You are centered, floating in stillness, beyond the grasp of worldly troubles.

The message of peace spreads outward with the light, flowing far beyond your physical being. The orange-golden glow radiates into the world, like a gentle invitation for others to find the same harmony within themselves. You are now the embodiment of peace - balanced, whole, complete. There is no more striving, no more yearning. In this stillness, everything aligns. Nothing can disturb you. You have found your center, and it shines quietly, like the first light of dawn breaking over the horizon.

Here, in this state of profound stillness, you rest. The golden ball hums softly within you, a reminder of the peace that is always present, waiting to be rediscovered. Beyond all suffering, beyond all fleeting emotions, you are here - whole, serene, eternal. By this point, you may drift into a deep slumber, a gentle indication that the meditation has fulfilled its purpose.

Having someone read this meditation flow to you, or committing it to memory and practicing it yourself, can be profoundly calming. In addition to the various meditation practices that necessitate carving out time from our hectic schedules, there exists a remarkably simple and accessible method of meditation. To truly grasp this approach, we must first understand the essence of meditation itself.

At its core, meditation is rooted in the concept of "dhyana," which emphasizes concentrating on a single object or point while gently setting aside the myriad of thoughts that often clutter our minds. This fundamental technique, as articulated by Osho, highlights that meditation can be seamlessly integrated into our daily lives and activities.

Osho suggests that this form of meditation is not confined to a quiet room or a specific time set aside for practice. Instead, it can be practiced while engaging in any task, whether it's washing the dishes, walking, or even working. The key is to really be in the moment, giving your full attention to whatever you're doing, and letting go of any distracting thoughts. When you do this, you start to feel more connected to the experience and become more aware of it, almost like you're in a calm, meditative state. This way of doing things turns even the simplest tasks into chances to be present and mindful, helping you find peace and clarity in the middle of daily chaos.

To help you understand this type of meditation, let me share an experience of mine. It began when I hurt my shoulder while working out. At first, I brushed it off, thinking it was just a minor sprain. As 3 days passed, the pain only worsened, and by the fourth day, it became unbearable. I decided to visit an orthopedic doctor. After examining me, he suspected a rotator cuff tear and recommended an MRI scan to get a clearer picture to guide the treatment process.

Now, I've always been terrified of MRI machines, and the thought of undergoing one made my heart race. So, I decided to rely on my willpower, convinced that I would heal on my own. For two months, I rested, applying ice packs to my shoulder. It seemed to improve a little, but then, out of nowhere, the pain flared up again. A sudden movement - one that I wasn't aware of - aggravated it, and this time, the pain was beyond unbearable. I realized that my initial hesitation could lead to something more serious, something I didn't want to ignore any longer. I gathered every ounce of courage I had and decided it was time to get the MRI.

The day of the scan, I was filled with nervous energy as I sat in the waiting room for what felt like an eternity, trying to quiet my mind. I kept telling myself, "It's just a machine.

You've got this. God is right here with you." But even as I repeated these reassuring words, my heart was racing. When my name was finally called, I was directed into the room where the scan would take place. The nurse handed me a loose, light blue cotton shirt and pants. Although the fabric was soft and comfortable, the tension in my body was still thick, growing heavier with each passing second.

As we approached the machine, my fear intensified. The sight of the large machine, surrounded by harsh lights, made my heart beat even faster. The technician instructed me to lie on the bed, placing a device on my left shoulder. He handed me a pump for emergencies, telling me to press it if something felt wrong. As I laid there, I closed my eyes, repeating to myself, "It's going to be alright. I'm not alone. God is with me." But when the bed started moving into the machine, a sense of darkness closed in, and panic surged within me. I felt as though the walls of the machine were swallowing me whole. My breath quickened, and in a state of sheer panic, I pushed the emergency button repeatedly.

The technician rushed to my side, his voice filled with concern. "Is everything alright?" he asked. Gasping for breath, I managed to say, "I'm claustrophobic. I don't think I can go back in." I could feel the weight of my fear bearing down on me, but then the nurse who had been assisting me returned. She spoke kindly, reminding me that it would only take 15 minutes, that I was stronger than I thought. Her gentle words offered some comfort, but it still took a few moments before I could calm myself enough to even speak.

Finally, I asked if they could play a bhajan (devotional song) - to soothe my nerves while I was inside the machine. The technician looked at me, understanding my distress, and agreed. He explained that I wouldn't be able to hear the song clearly due to the noise of the machine, but he would play it for me anyway. It was a Gujarati Krishna bhajan, *Ranchhod Rangila* - one that I'm never going to forget.

As the scan resumed, I was once again enveloped by the soft, familiar sounds of the bhajan. I focused entirely on the words, hearing them repeat in my ears like a gentle reminder that I wasn't alone. This time, my heart calmed, and my fear melted away. I was very calm throughout those 30 minutes of the scan. Yes! They were fooling me saying it will take 15 minutes. My entire attention during the scan was shifted to the words of the song - the words that soothed me.

When the scan was finally over, I emerged feeling peaceful. I realized that the key to my calm wasn't the avoidance of fear but the shift of my focus. In the beginning, I tried to suppress my fear, telling myself to be brave despite the rising panic. But when my attention shifted to the soothing repetition of the sacred song, the focus on my fear faded away. I wasn't fighting the claustrophobia anymore; I was simply immersed in the divine words, which provided the comfort I needed then.

Earlier my focus was on making myself not be scared

despite having the feeling in my heart that god is with me, my fear turned denser because of claustrophobia. However, when I had the holy name from the song constantly falling into my ear, I was consoled by it as now my attention had moved from claustrophobia to the holy name.This is precisely what the Osho meditation.

As a Krishn devotee, I often find myself drawn to the first type of meditation - immersing in the beauty of His divine form, which appears vividly before my closed eyes. On days when stress weighs me down, I turn to the breathing technique, allowing it to gently soothe and balance my inner world. Meanwhile, the golden ball meditation offers me a sense of liberation, helping me feel aligned with the divine essence. I practice all four methods, choosing intuitively which one resonates with me at any given moment. Each of them is equally soothing - you only need to select one to begin your journey inward.

For at its core, meditation is about cultivating an inner sanctuary where the divine and the mundane converge, allowing us to transcend our limitations and embrace our true essence.

Q16. What are the effects of meditation?

Meditation holds the key to unlocking physical well-being, emotional stability, and spiritual awakening. The transformative effects of meditation are vividly observed from the real-life instances of many great personalities. Across diverse paths, meditation reveals the same profound truth: it bridges the gap between the individual soul and the universal consciousness, leading to inner peace, self-realization, and liberation from suffering. As modern life grows increasingly fast-paced and stressful, the value of meditation becomes even more important, offering a peaceful escape and a way to bring balance back into our lives.

Beyond the Illusion of Self

Paramahansa Yogananda, the revered spiritual teacher encountered significant health challenges early in his life, particularly with recurring stomach ailments that plagued him for years. These struggles became pivotal in shaping not only his spiritual journey but also his profound teachings on meditation and self-realization.

In his early adulthood, Yogananda faced a particularly troubling period, beset by chronic stomach pain and digestive issues. This condition grew increasingly debilitating, affecting not just his physical health but also his spiritual practices and daily life. Despite his disciplined routine and earnest efforts to maintain his well-being, he found himself frequently incapacitated by these persistent health problems. Traditional remedies and medical treatments offered little solace, leading him to a state of frustration and despair.

During this tumultuous time, Yogananda sought the wisdom of his spiritual teacher, Swami Sri Yukteswar. Upon observing his disciple, Sri Yukteswar delivered a profound revelation that would change the course of Yogananda's life. He explained that Yogananda’s recurring illnesses were not merely physical ailments; rather, they were manifestations of his own mental and emotional turmoil. "It is you who are making yourself sick," Sri Yukteswar emphasized, "and it is you who can make yourself well." This striking insight marked a turning point for Yogananda, illuminating the significant role that thoughts and emotions play in one's physical health.

Following this enlightening encounter, Sri Yukteswar introduced Yogananda to the transformative practice of Kriya Yoga meditation. This technique was designed to cultivate deep inner peace and self-realization. With careful guidance, Sri Yukteswar instructed Yogananda to engage in regular meditation, focusing on his breath and harnessing the power of his mind. The practice aimed to promote profound awareness and relaxation, enabling Yogananda to release the underlying negative thoughts and emotions that had been contributing to his ailments.

Yogananda embraced this meditation practice wholeheartedly, integrating it into his daily routine with unwavering commitment. He began to witness a remarkable transformation. His stomach issues and frequent illnesses began to subside, leading him to a newfound state of health and vitality. The practice of meditation not only alleviated his physical discomfort but also nurtured a deep sense of inner peace and resilience.

This transformative experience profoundly influenced Yogananda's teachings. He emphasized the importance of self-awareness and the intrinsic mind-body connection, urging his students to understand how their thoughts and emotions could influence their physical health. Yogananda taught that through meditation and self-realization, individuals could cultivate balance and harmony in their lives, ultimately leading to improved health and well-being.

Yogananda's journey from chronic illness to vibrant health became a central theme in his life and teachings. He shared his story with others as an inspiration, illustrating the power individuals hold to take charge of their health and happiness through the transformative practice of meditation.

In essence, Yogananda's experience serves as a profound reminder of the impact of the mind on the body and the innate potential for healing that resides within each person. His teachings continue to inspire countless seekers on their spiritual journeys, illustrating the deep connection between meditation, health, and self-realization.

Rising Above Suffering: Goenka's Legacy

In the early 1960s, Goenka was a successful businessman in India, running a prosperous business in the field of manufacturing. However, he began to experience severe and debilitating migraines that made it increasingly difficult for him to function in his daily life. His health deteriorated to the point where he was unable to manage his business or enjoy life. Conventional medical treatments failed to provide relief, leaving him desperate for a solution.

During this difficult period, Goenka's life took a significant turn when he encountered the teachings of Vipassana meditation. Intrigued and hopeful, Goenka decided to immerse himself in this practice.

After attending a 10-day Vipassana meditation retreat, Goenka experienced a profound transformation. The meditation process allowed him to observe the sensations in his body and understand the nature of his mind, leading to a deep realization of impermanence and the importance of equanimity. As he practiced diligently, Goenka discovered that the meditation helped alleviate his migraines significantly. He learned to manage his pain through mindfulness and awareness, which helped him break free from the cycle of suffering caused by his condition (Goenka, n.d.).

Inspired by his healing experience, Goenka dedicated his life to teaching Vipassana meditation. He recognized the profound impact it had on his health and well-being, and he wanted to share this invaluable technique with others. In 1969, he established his first meditation center in India, and over the years, he expanded the movement globally, creating numerous meditation centers and retreats.

Goenka's approach to teaching Vipassana was rooted in the original teachings of the Buddha, focusing on the principles of mindfulness, insight, and the observation of bodily sensations. He emphasized the importance of self-discipline and the practice of equanimity, which he believed could lead individuals to profound inner peace and clarity.

Satya Narayan Goenka's journey from a health crisis to becoming a leading figure in the revival of Vipassana meditation is a testament to the healing power of meditation. His dedication to spreading this ancient practice has helped countless individuals find relief from various physical and mental ailments, transforming their lives in the process.

Through his efforts, Goenka not only healed his own health issues but also created a global community of practitioners who continue to benefit from the principles of Vipassana meditation. His legacy lives on in the meditation centers he established and in the thousands of individuals who have experienced healing and transformation through this powerful practice.

*

The ascetic yogis of the Himalayas demonstrate the transformative effects of long-term meditation. These sages live in seclusion, devoting their lives to spiritual practices. Their ability to survive harsh conditions, such as fasting or enduring extreme cold, is a testament to the mind-body control developed through meditation. These yogis enter states of samadhi - deep meditative absorption - where they experience a complete merging of the individual self with the divine. In these states, material desires dissolve, and only bliss and unity remain. While reaching that level of practice may not be easy for us, it is certainly not impossible (Das 2020).

यदा संहरते चायं कूर्मोऽङ्गानीव सर्वशः |
इन्द्रियाणीन्द्रियार्थेभ्यस्तस्य प्रज्ञा प्रतिष्ठिता || 2.58

{As a tortoise withdraws its limbs, a yogi must withdraw the senses from distractions to realize inner wisdom.}

The lives of these yogis show that meditation enables transcendence beyond fear, desire, and pain. Their stories inspire us to seek inner freedom and cultivate a connection with the inner divine amidst the distractions of the material world.

Another illustrative example is that of *Steve Jobs*, the co-founder of Apple Inc. Known for his innovation and visionary ideas. Jobs also struggled with intense stress and the pressures of his high-stakes career. To manage this, he turned to meditation, which became an integral part of his daily routine. Through mindfulness and meditation, Jobs cultivated a sense of clarity and focus that allowed him to tackle the challenges of his business with grace and insight.

Jobs often spoke about how meditation helped him tap into his creativity and problem-solving abilities, revealing how a peaceful mind can foster innovation. This practice also allowed him to approach his work with a renewed sense of purpose, unburdened by the anxieties that often accompany success. By embracing meditation, Jobs not only enhanced his own life but also positively influenced those around him, spreading a wave of inspiration and innovation.

Meditation has benefits that go beyond just the spiritual side, reaching the mind and body in real, practical ways. Research shows that meditation can help improve mental health, particularly in easing symptoms of anxiety, depression, and stress. Studies also reveal that regular meditation can change the structure of the brain, boosting the density of gray matter in areas that control emotions and self-awareness. For example, a study published in *Psychiatry Research* found that people who practiced mindfulness meditation showed less activity in the amygdala, the part of the brain that deals with fear and stress. This reduction in amygdala activity is linked to lower anxiety and better emotional health.

Meditation also helps improve important mental abilities like attention, memory, and decision-making. Studies, including one published in *Cognitive, Affective, & Behavioral Neuroscience*, have shown that mindfulness meditation can boost cognitive flexibility and working memory. For instance, a group of students who practiced mindfulness saw notable improvements in their academic performance compared to those who didn't meditate at all. This shows that meditation helps develop a focused and strong mind, which is crucial for handling the everyday challenges we face.

Meditation has been shown to have a number of physical health benefits, including lower blood pressure, a stronger immune system, and better sleep. One important study from *Harvard University* discovered that people who practiced meditation for just eight weeks experienced changes in their gene expression related to inflammation and stress (McGreevey 2013). This suggests that meditation can improve both mental health and physical health on a deeper, cellular level. For those dealing with chronic health issues like heart disease or diabetes, many report feeling much better and noticing improvements in their overall quality of life after adding meditation to their daily routine.

The benefits of meditation are not limited to mental and physical health; they also extend to spiritual fulfillment and personal growth. For those seeking deeper meaning, meditation offers a path to self-discovery. It helps individuals connect with their inner selves and align their lives with higher values and purpose.

नेहाभिक्रमनाशोऽस्ति प्रत्यवायो न विद्यते |

स्वल्पमप्यस्य धर्मस्य त्रायते महतो भयात् || 2.40

{On this path, no effort is ever wasted, and no failure exists; even the smallest step brings liberation.}

Some days, meditation may lead to blissful states of calm; on other days, it might simply bring a few moments of stillness amid chaos. But with consistency, the cumulative effects are transformative. As Yogananda explains, meditation allows us to rediscover our true nature - a state of joy, peace, and divine connection.

Whether practiced through Yogananda's Kriya Yoga, Vipassana's breath awareness, or the Himalayan yogis' austere methods, meditation offers a path to liberation from suffering. It nurtures mental clarity, emotional balance, and spiritual awakening. In today's hectic world, meditation serves as an anchor, helping us face challenges with grace and wisdom.

Meditation is more than a practice; it is a way of life - a

journey toward self-realization and inner freedom. Whether you are a beginner seeking stress relief or a spiritual seeker longing for enlightenment, meditation holds the power to transform your inner and outer world, one breath at a time. In a world increasingly dominated by distractions and pressures, meditation stands as a vital tool for reclaiming our health, happiness, and spiritual essence.

Q17. Does meditation remove or alter karmic impacts?

Meditation isn't just a practice; it's a journey that's deeply connected to our karma. It doesn't erase the effects of our past actions (prarabadh), but it helps us face them with more clarity and wisdom, guiding us through our karmic path. In the timeless wisdom of the Bhagavad Geeta, karma is seen as the law of action and reaction, a cosmic dance where every step leaves an imprint on our path. Each action we take is like a stone dropped in a vast ocean, influencing not only our current experiences but also those yet to come. Through meditation, we can begin to understand these waves more clearly, allowing us to choose our steps with intention.

तानि सर्वाणि संयम्य युक्त आसीत मत्परः।
वशे हि यस्येन्द्रियाणि तस्य प्रज्ञा प्रतिष्ठिता ॥ 2.61

{One who restrains his senses, keeping them under full control, and fixes his consciousness upon Me, is known as a man of steady intelligence.}

This insight strikes a deep chord, showing how meditation helps us take control of our senses and stay grounded in a clear and focused state. Imagine a candle flickering in a storm; when we focus our minds, we become that candle - steady and unwavering amid chaos. As we immerse ourselves in meditation, we discover a profound peace that can be addictive, enticing us to explore deeper realms of consciousness. This journey often transforms our very existence, guiding us to discern where to invest our energy. We start to recognize what nourishes our spirit and what drains it, shaping how we engage with the world around us.

The Turn of the Heart

Ahimsaka, once a nobleman, saw his life take a dark turn and became Angulimala. Raised in a well-to-do family, his mother envisioned him as a great scholar, sending him off to study. However, in the unforgiving halls of academia, he was ridiculed and shunned by his peers. Overwhelmed by humiliation and despair, Angulimala chose a path of crime, becoming a feared bandit notorious for his brutality. He earned the grim moniker "Angulimala," or "finger garland," for his heinous practice of collecting the fingers of his victims as trophies.

One fateful day, word reached Angulimala of a wandering ascetic known as Buddha, who preached love, compassion, and the cessation of suffering. Driven by a twisted desire to confront the enlightened one, Angulimala set out to claim Buddha's finger as his next trophy. But as he sprinted through the forest, no matter how fast he ran, he could not catch up. In a miraculous display of meditative power, Buddha remained serene, untouched by Angulimala's violent intentions.

Finally, face-to-face with Buddha, Angulimala barked, "Stop!" But the enlightened one calmly replied, "I have stopped, Angulimala. It is you who must stop." This modest yet deeply moving statement struck Angulimala to his core, unsettling the violent world he had built around himself. For the first time, he recognized the suffering he had inflicted - not just on others, but also upon himself.

Overcome with remorse, Angulimala pleaded for guidance and, with Buddha's blessing, embraced the path of meditation and Dharma. As he delved deep into meditation, Angulimala experienced a radical transformation. Through dedication and practice, he began to dissolve the weight of his past, relinquishing the violent urges that once defined him. The very fabric of his being shifted. Angulimala no longer sought to harm; instead, he found purpose in compassion and service. The karmic chains that had bound him to a life of violence began to unravel, revealing a path of peace. No longer remembered as a fearsome murderer, he became a venerated monk, embodying the principles of love and forgiveness.

योगसन्न्यस्तकर्माणं ज्ञानसञ्छिन्नसंशयम्।
आत्मवन्तं न कर्माणि निबध्नन्ति धनञ्जय ॥ 4.41

{One who acts in devotional service, renouncing the fruits of his actions, and whose doubts have been destroyed by transcendental knowledge, is situated factually in the self. Thus, he is not bound by the reactions of work, O conqueror of riches.}

Here it is revealed that through meditation, we can renounce our attachment to outcomes. Imagine standing at the edge of a vast field, where each action we take is a seed planted in the soil of our lives. With meditation, we learn to nurture these seeds without clinging to their growth, understanding that we can only control our efforts, not the results.

This practice encourages us to shift our focus from external validation to inner fulfillment. When we dedicate ourselves to the path of self-realization, we gradually unearth the essence of who we are beyond our actions and their consequences. The transformative nature of meditation allows us to transcend the immediate effects of our karmic debts, giving rise to a profound sense of liberation and thus living no interest in materialism leading to transformed behavior which in turn leads to diminishing karmic piles since you longer make new karmas.

यस्त्वात्मरतिरेव स्यादात्मतृप्तश्च मानवः।

आत्मन्येव च सन्तुष्टस्तस्य कार्यं न विद्यते॥ 3.17

{But for one who takes pleasure in the self, whose human life is one of self-realization, and who is satisfied in the self only, fully satiated - for him there is no duty.}

This encapsulates the essence of meditation: the deeper we delve into our inner selves, the less we are driven by external desires or the karmic debts of our past actions. As we become satiated with our own essence, we find that we no longer feel compelled to chase after fleeting rewards or validations, liberating ourselves from the shackles of karma.

The profound realization that arises through meditation leads us to make conscious choices, gradually aligning our actions with our values. This alignment not only affects our karmic patterns but also enhances our overall well-being. By omitting unnecessary karmas - those driven by ego, greed, or fear - we create a more harmonious existence. Through the lens of meditation, we learn to cultivate self-control and awareness. As we meditate regularly, we begin to notice the subtle shifts in our thoughts, emotions, and reactions. This steadiness allows us to handle life's challenges without becoming ensnared by the consequences of our actions.

यथा दीपो निवातस्थो नेड़ते सोपमा स्मृता।

योगिनो यतचित्तस्य युञ्जतो योगमात्मन: ॥ 6.19

{As a lamp in a windless place does not waver, so the transcendentalist, whose mind is controlled, remains always steady in his meditation on the transcendent self.}

In essence, while meditation might not wipe the slate clean initially, it provides a transformative lens through which we can view and interact with our karmic patterns. It cultivates self-awareness, emotional resilience, and inner peace, enabling us to rise above the immediate consequences of our actions. By nurturing a mindful practice, we learn to engage with life more consciously, crafting a path toward spiritual growth and liberation.

Ultimately, meditation serves as a gentle reminder that we are not merely products of our past; we are the architects of our future. Through this sacred

practice, we can alter the framework of our karmic debts, embracing a life that resonates with purpose, clarity, and profound inner freedom. As we cultivate this inner space of tranquility, we find ourselves not just living but thriving - free to create the reality we desire while remaining anchored in the wisdom of the present moment yet unaffected.

नेव तस्य कृतेनार्थो नाकृतेनेह कश्चन।

न चास्य सर्वभूतेषु कश्चिदर्थव्यपाश्रयः ॥ 3.18

{A self-realized man has no purpose to fulfill in the discharge of his prescribed duties, nor has he any reason not to perform such work. Nor has he any need to depend on any other living being.}

Q18. Is it really possible to nullify your karmic account in the present life?

This kind of doubt often crosses a person's mind in two situations: either when they're going through extreme struggles in life despite knowing they haven't done anything to deserve such hardship, or when they're aware of certain harsh actions they've taken in the present and now feel troubled, fearing the consequences of those choices.

Rebirth of the Broken

Shefali, a 39-year-old woman, had always struggled to find love in her life. Despite being talented and beautiful, she never found a partner who truly matched her. Life dealt her a hard blow when her father, whom she deeply adored, passed away when she was just sixteen. After his death, her mother moved with Shefali and her elder sister to live at her brother's (maternal uncle) house.

It was there that Shefali completed high school, but the environment was far from nurturing. She felt suffocated by constant domination and criticism from family members over the smallest things. Though she was still grieving her father's loss, she had to stay strong for her mother, especially since her elder sister was emotionally fragile.

Deep inside, Shefali was shattered, feeling the ache of her father's absence at every turn. Yet, through her pain, she built herself up to be strong, ready to face the battles life threw her way.

She managed to finish high school despite the chaos at home and the hardships she endured. The moment she turned 18, she moved out of her uncle's house with her mother and sister. Juggling part-time work, her studies, and caring for her widowed mother, she still found a way to save small amounts of money. With that, she invested in herself, learning new skills that not only made her independent but also helped her become a well-regarded individual.

Her dedication paid off when, at the age of 28, she achieved the incredible milestone of buying her own house, giving her mother the comfort and security of a home they could call their own. By then, her elder sister was married and had a four-year-old daughter. Despite a stable career and a loving family, she couldn't shake off a sense of emptiness - she yearned for a partner to share her life with.

She dated, but it didn't seem to click. In her search, some men didn't match her mindset, while others were only interested in casual relationships. In a world chasing fleeting connections, she longed for something deeper - an emotional bond. Time passed, and as she turned 30, she was still single. But just two months after her milestone birthday, she met a man who immediately captured her heart.

Things started off well between them. They enjoyed each other's company, and she supported him in every way she could. Having been through her own share of ups and downs, she approached love with sensitivity and strength. She firmly believed that relationships weren't just about one partner carrying the burden. Her philosophy was clear - love meant being a giver when needed, not just a receiver.

The year they spent together was anything but smooth; it felt like a rollercoaster ride. Yet, despite the challenges, she embraced it wholeheartedly as long as her efforts kept the relationship going. She loved deeply, pouring herself into the connection, hoping it would lead to the lasting companionship she desired.

At first, the relationship felt mutual, but over time, it became one-sided, with Shefali giving more than she was receiving. She noticed his changing behavior and how he pulled away, but she stayed quiet, thinking maybe he just needed space. She kept loving him the same way, hoping things would get better. One day, out of the blues, she found out he had been talking to and meeting another girl. She couldn't believe it, not because she didn't trust him, but because her faith in his appealing innocence had been so strong. Still, there was a voice inside her telling her to look deeper. Sadly, she discovered he had been cheating on her. When she confronted him with this, instead of apologizing, he argued with her and even abused her. At her age, with plans to marry him, she never expected to feel the kind of heartbreak a teenager might go through. It broke her, but she had to hold herself together.

She felt awful - unloved, unworthy, unattractive, and incomplete. Not having a loving partner made her question her worth. Her love for him was so deep that despite this betrayal, she couldn't stop thinking about him. Every day, she waited and prayed for him to come back, but he never even bothered to drop a heartfelt apology. What shocked her the most was that, despite knowing his mistakes, he never once took a moment to genuinely talk to her once. Six months had passed, yet she still longed for him. Her self-doubt grew so intense that she started to believe it might be the result of her past actions, something from her karma that was playing out in this situation.

From her young age, she was spiritual. After this separation from her partner, she didn't walk the path of modern casual hookups just to fulfil her the absence of a partner temporarily but took God's shelter. She started worshiping deeply just to have this man back. Very curiously, she wanted to know if, with the help of her worship, she could telepathically transform him. She didn't get her answer initially, but her faith in God kept her going. However, she came to know many other things about him which now finally made her move on from a person like him. Now, she worships deeply, but to keep herself grounded, grow in her spiritual journey, and be closer to God not to fulfil a wish of getting someone back. But the question still remains unanswered while she has turned 41. As a result of her dedication to her spiritual path, she no longer struggles with feelings of worthiness and has left it to God's hands to whether bless her with a loving partner or just make her his loving devotee for the rest of her life.

The motive of depicting this story here is to demonstrate a person's frustration which leads to such thoughts that makes them doubt if they had taken harsh actions (karma) previously, just as described in the beginning of this chapter. Now the question emerges is "what to do if such doubt arises in our minds?". The only answer to this is "Krishn" - The Only Savior. (There are many other ways to liberate, besides yoga sadhna, several tantric worships such as Dashmahavidya to liberate your soul, but those are not recommended to normal people like us because these sadhanas require our chakras to be open as well as high energetic potential to absorb such high intensity energy.)

Shrimad Bhagavata Mahapurana indeed emphasizes that worshiping Lord Krishn in any form can lead to the liberation of the soul. This concept is deeply rooted in the idea of bhakti, or devotion, which is central to many of Krishn's teachings. The text states that those who sincerely worship Krishn can attain spiritual liberation and ultimately return to the divine realm, thus escaping the cycle of birth and death.

In the Bhagavad Geeta, Lord Krishn teaches that while karma shapes our lives, it is not an irreversible force. Through deep devotion and surrender to God, one can transcend the effects of past actions. As stated in the verse below, those who dedicate themselves to different paths are drawn to corresponding deities, but those who surrender to the Supreme Divine, to Krishn, will attain liberation.

यान्ति देवव्रता देवान्पितॄ न्यान्ति पितृव्रताः ।

भूतानि यान्ति भूतेज्या यान्ति मद्याजिनोऽपि माम् ।। 9.25

{Worshippers of the celestial gods take birth amongst the celestial gods, worshippers of the ancestors go to the ancestors, worshippers of ghosts take birth amongst such beings, and My devotees come to Me alone.}

This verse highlights an important truth: by dedicating ourselves to devotion and selfless action, we can overcome the karmic ties that keep us trapped in the cycle of birth and rebirth. When we align our actions with God's will and offer everything we do as service to Him, we release ourselves from the hold of past karma. The Geeta teaches us that while we can't completely erase our karma, we can rise above its influence and move toward spiritual freedom, where our past actions no longer control our future.

It's not about renouncing life or escaping responsibilities that help us break free from karma, but about living with sincere devotion, acting selflessly, and surrendering the results of those actions to God. By following this path, we can free ourselves from the chains of karma and move toward the ultimate goal - union with the divine.

In the Bhagavata Purana, many parts explain how devotion to Krishn can transform a person's life. It shows that sincere worship can free someone from the struggles and attachments of the material world and help them realize their true spiritual self. This reflects the core belief that through devotion to Krishn, a person can rise above their karma and experience lasting peace and unity with the divine. In simple terms, both the Bhagavata Purana and the Bhagavad Geeta teach that truly dedicating oneself to Krishn can dissolve karma and lead to spiritual freedom in this lifetime.

According to sacred scriptures, we are granted this human form primarily to nullify our karmic debts either through the worship of Krishn or by becoming immersed in his divine name. This perspective underscores the significance of devotion as a pathway to redemption, emphasizing that engaging in bhakti(devotion) not only purifies the soul but also provides the opportunity to transcend the cycle of birth and rebirth. In this light, our human existence is seen as a precious chance to connect with the divine, facilitating our journey toward spiritual fulfillment.

This surrender need not be complicated. It can manifest in various ways: admiring Krishn's eternal beauty, immersing in His leela (divine play), listening to stories of His incarnations, or chanting His name in simple devotion - one of the most powerful practices. The repetition of His divine name itself holds so much power. The Geeta emphasizes that chanting Krishn's name works miracles - even when we don't fully understand how. The vibration of His name carries immense cleansing power, lifting burdens we didn't even know we carried.

METHOD OF WORSHIP

Q19. What is a better approach - idol worship or meditation?

India is a land of diverse religions and spiritual practices, each offering unique pathways to experience the divine. Among these, idol worship and meditation stand out as two prominent methods through which individuals seek a connection with God. While idol worship allows for a tangible representation of divinity, meditation emphasizes introspection and inner realization. Each approach has its own merits, and the choice between them often depends on personal beliefs and spiritual inclinations. While this question has possibly been one of the most debated in India throughout the years. I aim to answer it without bias, considering all aspects surrounding it.

In India, where 79.8% of the population identifies as Hindu, idol worship forms the heartbeat of faith for many. Yet, despite its deep-rooted presence, those who see the divine within a rock or metal statue are often met with skepticism. To me, such questioning feels misplaced. If something helps you connect with the sacred and keeps you grounded, why scrutinize it? Whether it's an idol or meditation, if it nurtures you and inspires personal growth, its essence should be honored, not dissected.

An idol, after all, is simply a creation of earthly elements – metals, stones, and minerals – mirroring the way our own bodies are woven from the five fundamental elements, the Panchmahabhuta: earth, water, fire, air, and ether. The only difference between a human body, fashioned by God, and a man-made idol of God lies in the presence of the soul, Praan. Just as life within us flickers out when the soul departs, an idol comes alive through the sacred ritual of Praan Pratishtha. This ceremony breathes divine energy into the statue, transforming it into more than mere metal or stone, a vessel capable of channeling blessings – though unlike us, it does not walk, speak, or move (Times of India 2024).

One of the most intriguing phenomena accompanying Praan Pratishtha is the spontaneous breaking of a mirror placed before the deity – an event unexplained by science to this day. Our ancestors believed that the mirror shatters when praanic energy floods into the idol, just as a soul enters or leaves a human body. For me, this mysterious act is proof enough that some divine force inhabits these forms. The deity in the idol sees us, hears us, and blesses us.

In moments of solitude, grief, or despair, when no one seems to listen, many of us find solace by sitting before an idol, pouring our hearts out. It is not the material statue that comforts us, but the presence we feel – one that understands, listens, and offers quiet relief. If something so simple brings peace to the soul, why question it? To feel heard, to feel blessed – isn't that the very essence of faith?

The spiritual fabric of India is richly adorned with practices that offer pathways to the divine. Idol worship, or *murti puja*, is deeply rooted in Indian culture and tradition. Temples across the country are adorned with exquisite idols, each meticulously crafted to embody various deities. This practice is not merely a ritual; it is an intricate art form that reflects devotion, creativity, and spirituality.

अनन्याश्चिन्तयन्तो मां ये जना: पर्युपासते |
तेषां नित्याभियुक्तानां योगक्षेमं वहाम्यहम् || 22||

{There are those who always think of Me and engage in exclusive devotion to Me. To them, whose minds are always absorbed in Me, I provide what they lack and preserve what they already possess.}

Devotion, whether through worshiping an idol or through other forms leads to a deeper connection with the divine. It underscores the importance of sincerity and love in worship, aligning well with the practice of idol worship as a means to express devotion.

Idol worship often serves as a medium through which devotees express their emotions and establish a connection with the divine. For example, a devotee of Lord Ganesha looks forward to the joy and comfort that Ganesh Chaturthi brings every year. She decorates her home with a beautiful idol of Ganesha, offers prayers, and makes sweets, turning it into a family tradition that brings everyone closer. For her, this ritual is more than just an act of devotion; it's a way to celebrate her heritage, with the presence of the idol helping her focus on feelings of gratitude and happiness.

Many individuals find solace and healing in the energy of temples, especially during significant festivals. A man recovering from a serious illness recounts his experiences visiting his local temple to worship the idol of Goddess Durga. During the Navaratri festival, he feels enveloped by a nurturing and protective energy that bolsters his spirit. The communal rituals performed in front of the idol provide him with divine support during his recovery, underscoring the power of collective devotion in healing.

Idol worship can also serve as a means for individuals to seek guidance in their lives. A woman faced with a challenging career decision turns to the idol of Goddess Saraswati, revered for wisdom and knowledge. By praying and lighting incense before the idol, she cultivates a sense of clarity and focus that aids her decision-making process. This ritual becomes a grounding practice that aligns her thoughts and feelings, connecting her to a higher power that guides her choices.

From a psychological perspective, the physical act of

bowing before an idol and offering prayers can create a sense of humility and reverence. This interaction serves as a reminder of the divine qualities one aspires to embody. Moreover, idol worship can be a communal experience, fostering a sense of belonging among devotees who gather to celebrate their faith.

यो मां पश्यति सर्वत्र सर्वं च मयि पश्यति ।
तस्याहं न प्रणश्यामि स च मे न प्रणश्यति || 30||

{For those who see Me everywhere and see all things in Me, I am never lost, nor are they ever lost to Me.}

The verse emphasizes that the divine is omnipresent and can be accessed through various forms, including idols. Though some may regard idol worship as purely symbolic, it acts as a meaningful practice for channeling devotion and concentrating the mind on the divine. Yet the architecture of temples enhances the spiritual experience. The *garbh griha* is often aligned with the cardinal directions and constructed using specific materials that are thought to store and radiate energy from the crown (top structure) of the temple channelizing directly to the higher energy present in the universe to the devotees ("Temple Architecture – Devalaya Vastu – Part Five (5 of 9)" 2012). This creates an environment where devotees can feel the divine energy as they engage in worship. The energy experienced in these temple centers is protective, nourishing, and warm, often bringing comfort to the worshiper.

On the other hand, meditation invites practitioners to embark on an inward journey, transcending the need for external representations of divinity. It is a practice rooted in the belief that the essence of God resides within each individual. Through meditation, one aims to quiet the mind and connect with this inner divinity. The belief that *"the whole universe is within us"* can be experienced through profound states of meditation.

Meditation encourages self-reflection, leading to personal growth and a deeper understanding of oneself. It teaches practitioners to observe their thoughts without attachment, cultivating a sense of inner peace and tranquility. The energy experienced during meditation is tranquilizing, providing a calming effect that helps individuals face the challenges of life.

चञ्चलं हि मन: कृष्ण प्रमाथि बलवद्दृढम् |
तस्याहं निग्रहं मन्ये वायोरिव सुदुष्करम् || 34||

{The mind is restless, turbulent, obstinate, and very strong;
O Krishn, and to subdue it is more difficult than
controlling the wind.}

This acknowledgment of the mind's challenges is crucial for those who seek to embark on a meditative path. Through regular practice, however, one can learn to harness the mind's energy and achieve a state of equilibrium.

While idol worship and meditation may seem contradictory, they can coexist harmoniously within one's spiritual practice. For many, idol worship serves as a preliminary step toward deeper spiritual exploration. The tangible connection to the divine through idols can help focus the mind and heart, creating fertile ground for the more abstract practice of meditation.

In my belief, both methods offer valuable pathways to connect with the divine and experience spiritual growth. Rather than viewing them as opposing practices, it may be more fruitful to appreciate how they can complement each other, enriching the spiritual journey.

ये यथा मां प्रपद्यन्ते तांस्तथैव भजाम्यहम् |
मम वर्त्मानुवर्तन्ते मनुष्याः पार्थ सर्वशः || 11||

{In whatever way people surrender unto Me, I reciprocate accordingly. Everyone follows My path, knowingly or unknowingly, O son of Pritha.}

This verse indicates that different forms of worship,

whether idol worship or meditation, are all valid ways to reach the divine. Ultimately, spirituality is not about choosing the "right" path but about embracing the path that embraces our soul. Because,

न देवो विद्यते काष्ठे न पाषाणे न मृण्मये ।

भावे हि विद्यते देवस्तस्माद्भावो हि कारणम् ॥

{God cannot be found in a wood piece, stone or a mud idol. It is the belief that makes us feel the presence of God. Hence, only the feeling matters - not the material.}

\- समयोचितपद्यरत्नमालिका

Q20. Is sorrow originally a medium to self-contentment?

In the journey of life, success is often shaped by struggles and challenges, with sorrow being one of the most profound teachers along the way. Many who now stand tall in the light of their achievements began as ordinary people, grappling with life's heart-wrenching moments, at times feeling as though their world had shattered. Behind every triumph, there is a story of struggle, a reminder that the journey to self-contentment is not easy, and often, sorrow itself serves as the medium through which this transformation occurs.

Sorrow, when met with acceptance and introspection, has the potential to become a powerful catalyst for personal growth and spiritual understanding. Rather than viewing it as something to avoid or overcome, we can learn to see sorrow as an invitation to look deeper within ourselves. In those painful moments, when life feels at its most broken, we are given the opportunity to explore our innermost fears, desires, and wounds. This process of introspection can lead to deep healing and insight, helping us to understand not only who we are but also who we are meant to become.

Through this lens, sorrow becomes less of a burden and more of a guide, leading us toward greater self-awareness and, ultimately, self-contentment.

The stories of those who have struggled and emerged victorious remind us of something powerful and universal: success is never handed over easily. It demands unwavering determination, the strength to keep pushing forward despite the weight of failure, and the courage to rise again, no matter how many times we fall. But even with all this effort, there are times when our spirits falter, and the flame of motivation that once burned bright begins to flicker and fade. We start to doubt ourselves, questioning why we try so hard when it feels like nothing is changing.

In these moments, it takes a deep, unwavering faith to hold on. It takes a steadfast belief that there's more to our journey than what meets the eye - that the universe, in all its complexity, has a plan for us. Even when everything feels uncertain, when the path ahead seems unclear, we must trust in the timing of the universe and the will of a higher power, knowing that every experience, every struggle, and every setback is part of the greater design guiding us forward.

From Sorrow to Serenity: Ananda's Journey to Enlightenment

Ananda, one of the Buddha's most devoted disciples, shared a bond with his teacher that was both intimate and profound. He had stood by the Buddha's side throughout his life, faithfully absorbing the teachings and offering support, especially during the Buddha's final days. For Ananda, the Buddha was not only a guide but also a close friend and the ultimate source of wisdom. So, when the Buddha passed away, Ananda was consumed by a deep, overwhelming sorrow. It was as if a part of him had been torn away, leaving a gaping emptiness in its place.

This sorrow was not merely an emotional loss; it was a spiritual crisis. Ananda found himself wrestling with the very teachings the Buddha had imparted - lessons on impermanence and suffering. How could he reconcile these truths with the crushing weight of his grief? For a long time, Ananda questioned his ability to continue on the spiritual path without the Buddha's physical presence to guide him.

Yet, it was in the depth of this sorrow that Ananda's true spiritual awakening began. As he sat alone in meditation, grappling with his grief, a realization began to unfold. Ananda saw that his suffering stemmed from attachment - the very attachment the Buddha had warned against. His sorrow was rooted in his unwillingness to accept the impermanence of all things, even the Buddha himself. In that painful moment of truth, Ananda understood: everything, even the most cherished of beings, must eventually depart. True liberation could not be found in holding onto the past or clinging to the physical form of the Buddha. The path to peace lay in embracing impermanence.

Through this acceptance, Ananda's sorrow began to shift. It transformed from a burden into a profound opportunity for growth. As he embraced the Buddha's teachings of non-attachment and impermanence, his heart lightened. The grief that had once overwhelmed him now became a catalyst for deeper understanding and spiritual peace.

By the end of that night, Ananda had attained enlightenment. No longer did he cling to the Buddha's physical presence; instead, he realized that the true legacy of the Buddha was found in the teachings he had left behind. The sorrow that had once seemed insurmountable had become the fertile ground from which wisdom and inner peace grew.

*

Patience is a virtue that many of us struggle to truly embrace. As the years unfold, it's easy to fall into the trap of comparisons, constantly measuring our journey against those of others. We look at friends, colleagues, or acquaintances - people who once seemed to be walking the same path as us - and see them standing taller, higher on the ladder of success, basking in the glow of their achievements. It's a painful contrast, one that can sting deeply and leave us questioning our own worth. We see them effortlessly reaping the rewards of their hard work, while we toil and sweat, pouring ourselves into every task, only to watch our efforts yield what feels like little more than scraps. The fruits of our labor seem small, insignificant, and the weight of that perceived failure only grows heavier. The joy of accomplishment feels just out of reach, and instead of progress, we're left with a sense of inadequacy, wondering why the universe seems to favor others over us. The more we try, the deeper the sense of despair can grow, as though we're stuck in a cycle, while the world around us moves on.

From this discontent arises an invaluable lesson: life unfolds at its own pace, with success arriving in its own time. Just as one person may flourish today, so too will we - when our moment arrives. However, fixating on what others have achieved often distracts us from recognizing the divine plan unfolding in our lives. This preoccupation leads us to question our next steps, seeking shortcuts to results that, if they come too quickly, may not serve us in the long run.

In those moments when the universe seems to conspire against us, and fatigue from unyielding effort settles into our bones, we must summon the strength to remain patient. It is in these trying times that the key to success reveals itself: patience. The path may feel arduous and devoid of reward, yet we must remind ourselves that this struggle is merely a precursor to the blossoming that awaits. Like a seed buried in darkness, the journey may be tough, but it will yield beauty beyond measure.

Consider the story of Shefali, who faced sorrow following the end of a cherished relationship. At first, the pain felt insurmountable, an ache that gnawed at her spirit. However, when she channeled that sorrow constructively, it transformed into a source of strength and joy. Every trial that draws us closer to the divine, even those that wound us, is a worthy endeavor.

यत्तदग्रे विषमिव परिणामे5मृतोपमम्।

तत्सुखं सात्त्विकं प्रोक्तमात्मबुद्धिप्रसादजम् ॥ 18.37

{That which in the beginning may be just like poison but at the end is just like nectar and which awakens one to self-realization is said to be happiness in the mode of goodness.}

What may initially appear as poison can ultimately yield the sweetest nectar. This happiness, born from self-realization, is the essence of goodness. As we journey through life, we may discover that, despite delayed results, our struggles were not in vain. The effort expended in pursuit of our goals, while seemingly unfruitful at times, often leads us to outcomes that exceed our wildest imaginations. Yet, we must also acknowledge the other side of success; those who once stood tall in wealth and stability may face a decline, their fortunes waning over time.

विषयेन्द्रियसंयोगाद्यत्तदग्रेऽमृतोपमम्।
परिणामे विषमिव तत्सुखं राजसं स्मृतम्॥ 18.38

{That happiness which is derived from contact of the senses with their objects and which appears like nectar at first but poison at the end is said to be of the nature of passion.}

The happiness derived from fleeting pleasures may shine brightly at first, resembling nectar, yet can ultimately turn bitter, much like poison. Such joy, steeped in passion, is ephemeral, highlighting the importance of discerning the nature of our pursuits.

The duality of success and failure teaches us profound lessons. The winds of change are constant, and with them comes the realization that our paths may be winding and uncertain. However, with each twist and turn, we are invited to deepen our understanding of patience and resilience. Each setback is a stepping stone, guiding us closer to our true selves.

As we cultivate our dreams, we must nurture them with love and care. Our aspirations demand more than mere effort; they require belief in the unseen forces at play. With patience, we allow the universe to orchestrate our journeys. In the stillness of waiting, we can hear the whispers of divine timing, gently urging us to trust the process.

We can take inspiration from the natural world, where growth occurs beneath the surface long before it bursts into bloom. The seasons remind us of the cyclical nature of life; what lies dormant today may flourish tomorrow. Embracing this rhythm encourages us to approach our struggles with grace, viewing them as opportunities for growth rather than barriers to our success.

In the quiet moments, when doubt creeps in and shadows loom large, we can turn inward and reconnect with our intentions. It is essential to remind ourselves that we are not alone in our journeys. Every individual experiences the weight of uncertainty, yet it is how we respond to these challenges that shapes our destinies.

As we move through our journeys, let us recognize our accomplishments, no matter how minor or major, and value the lessons we've derived from our challenges. Each experience, whether joyous or painful, contributes to the mosaic of our lives. In moments of reflection, we can acknowledge the beauty in our struggles, recognizing that they are integral to our growth.

Patience is not a passive state; it is an active choice, a commitment to continue striving despite the odds. It invites us to cultivate resilience and hope, to trust that our efforts will bear fruit in due time. With this mindset, we can transform our experiences into stepping stones, propelling us toward our dreams.

While embracing the truth that success is not merely a destination but a continuous process of growth and self-discovery is also essential. Just as Shefali learned to harness her pain, we too can channel our experiences into something transformative. The journey may be challenging, but it is also a pathway to enlightenment, leading us to a deeper connection with ourselves and the universe.

Since, individuals who possess a deep sense of self-contentment often discover the pinnacle of success, as their inner fulfillment drives them to pursue their goals with unwavering passion and purpose. This intrinsic satisfaction enables them to overcome challenges with resilience, allowing them to reach heights that may elude those who lack such inner peace.

In the end, we must remind ourselves that every effort, every moment of patience, is worth the wait. Like the flowers that bloom after a long, harsh winter, our lives will flourish when we remain steadfast in our belief. Embrace the journey, for it is in the waiting that we often find our greatest strength.

Q21. What is self-realization and its importance?

We've often heard the phrase, "We are born alone, and we will die alone." Yet, how often do we pause to reflect on this profound notion? In a world where companionship is sought after in every aspect of life, we often overlook the beauty of solitude. We cultivate friendships throughout our lives - at work, school, and in various social settings. We feel an inherent need to surround ourselves with others, even at the dinner table or during lunch breaks at work. Many of us prefer the company of friends while grabbing a quick bite, and if we find ourselves alone, we instinctively reach for our phones or turn on the television.

This phenomenon has transformed mealtime into a social networking session, where the act of eating has become secondary to scrolling through social media or binge-watching the latest show. With technology at our fingertips, the physical distance between family members has grown, and we rarely carve out precious time for ourselves. It has become increasingly challenging to find moments of solitude, where we can sit in silence and let our thoughts roam freely. The irony lies in the fact that while many young individuals are still able to spend quality time with loved ones, the constant pull of gadgets has deepened the chasm within families.

A well-meaning mother may believe she understands her child, yet remains oblivious to the hidden struggles that often lurk beneath the surface of his life. In modern households, it's common for every family member to occupy the same room, yet each person is lost in their own digital universe, oblivious to one another's presence. This situation may seem trivial, but when spiritual leaders or life coaches highlight the profound effects of this disconnect on our mental health, it becomes clear that this phenomenon is anything but benign.

In our pursuit of direction, especially when choosing a career path, we often seek guidance from professionals. These advisors typically offer insights based on our qualifications and the financial potential of different fields. However, their focus tends to be on the revenue we could generate rather than our genuine interests and passions. In my view, career choices should stem from what we love, what ignites our enthusiasm. When we choose a path aligned with our passions, work transforms from a chore into a source of fulfillment, and we find ourselves energized rather than fatigued.

This brings us to the vital concept of self-realization. To explore its significance, we must first understand what it truly means. The term can be broken down into two components: "self" and "realization." The first component suggests a focus solely on ourselves, while the second indicates an awakening to something deeper. In essence, self-realization is the act of sitting in solitude, free from distractions - no devices, no books - allowing thoughts to flow unimpeded. It's about accepting whatever arises in our minds, whether positive or negative, and simply being present with those thoughts.

When you first embark on this journey of self-realization, it's common to feel overwhelmed by the flood of thoughts that emerge. In today's fast-paced world, we've largely forgotten how to embrace our own thoughts. Instead of welcoming the natural flow of ideas, we often resort to distractions - food, television, or our phones. The omnipresence of social media compounds this issue, offering us an endless stream of content that keeps us entertained yet isolated. We've developed a habit of turning to our devices for stimulation, consuming mindless content that, despite its trivial nature, provides a false sense of engagement.

The Tale of the Wise King and the Mirror

Once upon a time, there was a wise king who ruled over a peaceful kingdom. One day, the king received a gift from a wandering sage - a beautifully crafted mirror. The king was intrigued and asked the sage how to use it.

The sage replied, "This mirror will show you your true self, not the reflection you see in your everyday mirror. But be warned, it will reveal everything: your fears, your desires, and your hidden truths."

Curious, the king gazed into the mirror. At first, he saw his reflection, just as he had always appeared - strong, regal, confident. But as he looked deeper, the mirror began to show him his insecurities, his pride, and the moments when he had acted out of anger rather than wisdom. He saw the flaws in his leadership and the mistakes he had ignored.

Shocked and unsettled, the king turned away. He asked the sage, "I don't want to see these truths. They make me uncomfortable."

The sage smiled gently and said, "The mirror only reflects what is already within you. Self-realization is not about avoiding discomfort, but about facing it and understanding it. Only by acknowledging your true self can you begin to change."

Over time, the king returned to the mirror, this time with an open heart. He faced his flaws, accepted his imperfections, and worked on becoming a wiser, kinder ruler. In doing so, he found true peace within himself and became the ruler his people admired, not for his power, but for his self-awareness.

*

The key is persistence. The practice of self-realization requires us to commit to sitting with our thoughts, regardless of how unsettling they may feel at first. As we continue this practice, it can evolve into a new addiction - a positive one. Gradually, we'll carve out moments of solitude amidst the noise of everyday life, finding solace in the tranquility that this practice brings. Over time, this journey can transport us to realms of awareness previously unexplored, cultivating a mindset akin to that of a monk.

Achieving this inner calm leads to newfound clarity. No longer will our minds be inundated with a chaotic stream of thoughts; instead, we'll gain a deeper understanding of what truly matters to us. This clarity empowers us to make choices that resonate with our authentic selves, freeing us from the burden of societal expectations. We won't be swayed by the paths others choose; we will carve our own.

बुद्धया विशुद्धया युक्तो धृत्यात्मानं नियम्य च।

शब्दादीन्विषयांस्त्यक्त्वा रागद्वेषो व्युदस्य च॥ 18.51

विविक्तसेवी लघ्वाशी यतवाक्कायमानसः ।

ध्यानयोगपरो नित्य वैराग्यं समुपाश्रितः॥ 18.52

अहङ्कारं बलं दर्प काम क्रोधं परिग्रहम्।

विमुच्य निर्ममः शान्तो ब्रह्मभूयाय कल्पते॥ 18.53

{Being purified by his intelligence and controlling the mind with determination, giving up the objects of sense gratification, being freed from attachment and hatred, one who lives in a secluded place, who eats little, who controls his body, mind and power of speech, who is always in trance and who is detached, free from false ego, false strength, false pride, lust, anger, and acceptance of material things, free from false proprietorship, and peaceful - such a person is certainly elevated to the position of self-realization.}

As we disconnect from external distractions, we elevate our consciousness to new heights. In solitude, we can sift through our thoughts and feelings, gaining insight into our true selves. This process helps us shed false ego, pride, and material attachments, allowing us to experience a deeper sense of peace and fulfillment.

In this journey of self-discovery, it's crucial to recognize the influence of the people we surround ourselves with. The company we keep can significantly impact our sense of self and our spiritual growth. While friendships can offer support and companionship, they can also feed into the false ego and distractions that hinder our journey toward self-realization. Toxic relationships may pull us into patterns of comparison, competition, or negativity, clouding our judgment and distorting our perceptions of success and happiness.

In many cases, it can be more beneficial to embrace solitude. By spending time alone, we create space for introspection and self-reflection, allowing us to connect deeply with our thoughts and feelings. Alone time grants us the freedom to explore our passions without external pressures. When we remove ourselves from the influence of others, we cultivate a stronger sense of self, which ultimately leads to greater clarity in our decisions and direction in life.

As we embark on this path toward self-realization, let us acknowledge the transformative power of solitude. By embracing moments of silence, we open ourselves to new insights and revelations. It is in these quiet moments that we can begin to understand our true desires and motivations, unclouded by the expectations and distractions of the world around us.

Ultimately, self-realization is not merely about solitude; it is a journey toward understanding ourselves on a deeper level. By quieting the noise and allowing our thoughts to flow, we create the opportunity for profound growth and transformation. The journey may be challenging, but the rewards of self-discovery are invaluable. In embracing this process, we can step into a life filled with purpose, authenticity, and a true connection to ourselves and the world around us.

Through the discipline of self-control and the art of solitude, we can free ourselves from the chains of ego and distraction. In doing so, we cultivate inner peace, allowing us to embrace our authentic selves with greater confidence. This newfound clarity guides us on a path where we can truly thrive - personally, professionally, and spiritually.

ATTACHMENT

Q22. How to accept the death of loved ones?

In a world brimming with both endless possibilities and daunting challenges, Smriti, a spirited 24-year-old, made a decision that would forever change the course of her life. Bright, ambitious, and athletically gifted, she had always been the beloved - perhaps a little spoiled - daughter of her family. But after finishing her Bachelor's degree, the call of the unknown tugged at her heart. She set her sights on the United States, knowing deep down that this was her chance to stretch beyond the familiar and embrace a future full of growth and opportunity. Saying goodbye to the comfort of home and the warmth of loved ones was no small feat, yet in this fast-paced world, the promise of new experiences and a brighter tomorrow seemed worth every sacrifice. With unwavering resolve, Smriti took a deep breath and stepped boldly onto a path of transformation, ready to see where it would lead her.

The first three months were a whirlwind of struggles. Everything was new - faces, places, work environments, and an emotional rollercoaster she hadn't quite prepared for. Yet, in this sea of change, she managed to grow more confident and independent with each passing day.

Meanwhile, on the other side of the world, her family felt the sting of her absence in every small moment of joy. Each celebration, no matter how cheerful, carried a faint shadow of longing - an empty chair at the table, a missing voice in their laughter, and a quiet ache that reminded them of the void she had left behind. Each gathering felt a little hollow, yet there was comfort in the unspoken understanding that she was flourishing - finding fulfillment in both her personal growth and professional success. Though they weren't together, they found peace knowing she was on her path, becoming the person she was meant to be.

In another part of the city, Aditi, a 28-year-old girl, immersed herself in the demanding world of a doctorate in pharmacy. Her life was filled with ambition and late-night study sessions, yet there was one constant that kept her grounded - her older brother, Dhruv - a practicing surgeon. At 34, Dhruv was not just her sibling, but her closest confidant and best friend.

Aditi had always been the pampered one, spoiled not just by her parents, but also by Dhruv. Her love for shopping was no secret; the thrill of buying new clothes and jewelry brought her a certain joy, a brief escape from the pressures of her studies. But the roots of her indulgence ran deeper - especially in the way her mother expressed her love. Her mother, who had always been her greatest supporter, showered Aditi with gifts, believing they were the best way to show her affection.

But beneath the surface of their warm, loving family, a quiet struggle lingered. Their mother, though strong and vibrant, was battling health issues - diabetes and hypertension that required constant care. Yet despite the challenges, the family thrived in harmony, finding strength in their love for one another, their bond unbreakable in the face of adversity.

Life had unfolded beautifully for both families, filled with hope and joy, until the world was shaken by the devastating wave of COVID-19 - a catastrophe that will haunt us for generations. Just five months after Smriti moved to the U.S., she received the heartbreaking news that her mother's health had taken a severe turn. The virus had ravaged her body, and she was now in the hospital, her oxygen levels plummeting, her life hanging by a thread. Smriti's heart sank as she learned that the hospitals, overwhelmed by the surge of patients, were unable to provide the care her mother so urgently needed. No matter how much they were willing to pay, securing a bed seemed impossible. The streets of India were overflowing with the suffering, and families were left in a state of anguish, desperate to save their loved ones. In a last-ditch effort to protect her mother from further infection, Smriti's family tried to create a makeshift care setup at home, but even that was futile. Oxygen cylinders - once a simple necessity - had become an unreachable lifeline. Their hope slowly turned to helplessness, and the fear of losing her mother loomed ever larger.

When Smriti learned of her mother's condition, it felt as though the ground beneath her feet had crumbled. She collapsed to the floor, her body refusing to accept the unbearable truth that her cherished mother was slipping away. In that agonizing moment, her heart shattered into a thousand pieces, and an overwhelming tide of grief consumed her. The thought of never seeing her mother again, of missing her final moments, gripped her like a vice, leaving her breathless and speechless. She withdrew into herself, retreating from the world as the weight of sorrow pressed down on her chest. The days that followed were nothing but a blur - time seemed to lose its meaning. She barely ate, barely drank, lost in a fog of despair. The emotional toll was profound, pushing her into isolation, distancing herself from friends and family who struggled to reach her.

But even in the depths of her darkness, Smriti found a glimmer of light in her friends across the U.S. They became her lifeline, offering her love and unwavering support when she needed it most. Two of them, sensing the depth of her pain, invited her to stay with them, wrapping her in their care and kindness. Yet, no matter how much they gave, Smriti's sorrow remained a heavy weight she couldn't lift. Her heart broke at the thought that she had missed the last moments with her mother - the sacred rituals, the last goodbyes, everything she so desperately wanted to be there for. The world around her felt unbearably cruel, like it had conspired against her. Flights were few and far between, jobs slipped from her grasp, and even if she managed to return home, the looming threat of quarantine for days would steal away the precious time she so desperately needed. It felt as if the walls of her world were closing in, and the sharp sting of helplessness gnawed at her, relentless and unyielding.

In an instant, Smriti's dreams felt like they had crumbled into dust. The vision of her wedding day, once so vivid, seemed impossible to hold onto - how could she picture herself stepping into the sacred space of the wedding (mandap) without her mother's reassuring presence beside her? The thought of marriage faded into the distance, swallowed by the weight of her grief. Yet, as the months slowly passed, a quiet transformation began within her. Smriti started to emerge from the suffocating darkness of sorrow, finding a flicker of light in her devotion to her Kanhaji. Every morning, she would light a lamp, sitting before her deity, her heart laid bare in the silence. With every prayer, every whispered word, she poured out her deepest feelings. This sacred bond became her sanctuary, the one thread of hope that guided her through the storm. It was through this connection with God that Smriti found the strength to face each new day, her heart slowly mending, piece by piece.

Simultaneously, Aditi's world was torn apart by tragedy. As Smriti's life was unraveling in one corner of the world, Aditi's life was shattering in another. Amid the chaos of the

COVID pandemic, her mother collapsed hitting her head while doing something as ordinary as household chores. Dhruv, who had just returned home from a long, exhausting shift, was the first to see her fall. As a doctor, he understood all too well the overwhelming strain on hospitals, the scarcity of resources, and the grave risks of exposing his already fragile mother to further harm. For a fleeting moment, he hoped she could make it through at home with his medical expertise. He set up a makeshift care station, doing what he could with the knowledge he had. But within the hour, reality hit - her condition was rapidly deteriorating, and there was no choice but to get her to a hospital.

With a heavy heart, Dhruv put his mother in the backseat of his car to drive her to the hospital and sent Aditi on a desperate mission to secure a bed, knowing full well that even his connections might not be enough in such a crisis. As they sped through the streets, the car was filled with an eerie stillness. Her mother, barely conscious, lying on his father's lap whispered soft, tender words into his ears, urging him to live joyfully for their children. Despite Dhruv's hope and his medical certainty that she might survive, her pale, lifeless form told another story. By the time they arrived at the hospital, she had already slipped away, leaving only the weight of unspoken words and an aching silence.

Aditi and Dhruv were shattered, their hearts heavy with the weight of their grief. Dhruv, especially, felt as though the ground beneath him had been ripped away. "What was the point of all my medical training if I couldn't save my own mother?" he questioned himself, the words cutting through him like a blade. For three endless nights, he was consumed by grief, his mind spiraling into darkness.

Aditi, too, was consumed by regret. She longed for the chance to have been by her mother's side in those final, precious moments, but now it was too late. The silence in their home was deafening, an empty echo where once there had been laughter and warmth. Even the most mundane tasks - things that once felt simple - felt impossible without her mother's comforting presence. Each passing moment was a reminder that something vital, something irreplaceable, was gone. Their world, once filled with love, had become a hollow shell, and they were left to navigate the crushing weight of their loss.

Death - the cold, inevitable end of life - strips us of our sense of security and leaves us feeling vulnerable. When we lose someone we love, a part of us feels like it's been torn away. In the silence that follows, we find ourselves questioning everything we once held certain, struggling to make sense of a world that feels emptier without them. The strength to heal, to gather the broken pieces of ourselves, seems almost out of reach, no matter how many comforting words surround us. Losing something precious, even just for a moment, shakes us to the core. But to lose a loved one forever - that is a sorrow so deep, it's hard to even fathom.

Both Smriti and Dhruv felt adrift, their sense of self shattered by the loss of their mothers' demise.

This pain stems from the powerful attachments we form in the close-knit relationships. It's a pain that tugs at the very core of who we are. It is thus, as we grow older, the need to understand detachment becomes more crucial. Grasping this concept is not about rejecting love, but learning to let go - embracing the balance between connection and freedom. In doing so, we equip ourselves with the resilience needed to face life's challenges, safeguarding our emotions amidst the inevitable storms of loss.

Emotional bonds with our family are deeply etched into us, like the roots of a tree that anchor it to the earth. Yet, in the midst of this love, there is quiet wisdom that urges us to cultivate a sense of detachment, understanding that separation is not just possible, but inevitable. Life itself, with its unending cycle of birth, death, and rebirth, serves as a gentle reminder of this truth. Though it may feel hard to grasp, there is a moving story from the Mahabharata that captures this reality perfectly.

Whispers of the Soul: Arjun and Abhimanyu's Divine Encounter

In the midst of this storm, it was Krishn, with his infinite compassion and wisdom, who reached out to Arjun, guiding him away from the chaos of his emotions. With a divine touch, Krishn led Arjun to a realm beyond the physical, a place where the soul of Abhimanyu awaited. There, in the timelessness of the soul's existence, Abhimanyu stood - his spirit untouched by the horrors of the battlefield, radiant and serene.

A wave of relief swept over Arjun as he saw his son once more, but it was quickly replaced by a sharp ache in his chest. Without hesitation, he rushed forward, yearning to hold him, to feel the warmth of his son's embrace. But as he reached out, Abhimanyu's words struck him like a thunderbolt: strange, unfamiliar, yet achingly familiar. "I'm sorry," he said, his tone laced with confusion. "I don't recognize you. Could you tell me who you are?"

It was as though the ground beneath Arjun's feet had crumbled. His heart, already broken, shattered again. The voice of his son, the one he had raised, now felt like the voice of a stranger. The pain was unbearable, and his thoughts became a blur of anguish. Desperation surged through him, and he turned to Krishn, seeking answers, yearning to understand why his son, who had once called him "father," now seemed so distant.

Krishn, with his eternal grace, revealed the deepest truth of existence. "When the soul leaves the body," he said softly, "it sheds all attachments, all memories of its earthly form." The soul is no longer bound by the identity it once held. It is free, untethered to the pain and grief that death brings to those who remain.

Arjun listened, his heart heavy with sorrow yet stirred by the compassion in Krishn's words. Krishn spoke of the eternal journey of the soul, a journey that transcends death, a journey that continues far beyond the fleeting moments of this world. "Do not mourn for the dead," Krishn urged, his voice a gentle balm to Arjun's wounded spirit. "Death is not an end, but a transition, a transformation. The soul, in its essence, can never be lost. It only changes."

At that moment, something within Arjun shifted. The weight of his sorrow, though still heavy, began to lift. He understood, on a deeper level, that death was not the end, but a part of an eternal cycle - a cycle of life, death, and rebirth. The essence of his son was not gone; it had simply moved on to another form. And though Arjun would carry the pain of separation, he knew that the soul of Abhimanyu, like his own, would forever be part of the divine journey.

अव्यक्तोऽयमचिन्त्योऽयमविकार्यो ऽयमुच्यते ।
तस्मादेवं विदित्वैनं नानुशोचितुमर्हसि ॥ 2.25

{It is said that the soul is invisible, inconceivable and immuable. Knowing this, you should not grieve for the body.}

अथ चेन नित्यजातं नित्यं वा मन्यसे मृतम्।
तथापि त्वं महाबाहो नैवं शोचितुमरर्हसि ॥ 2.26

{If, however, you think that the soul [or the symptoms of life] is always born and dies forever, you still have no reason to lament, O mighty-armed.}

*

In my belief it's vital to embrace the ultimate wisdom that Krishn offers us. I know that accepting this truth can feel daunting, even overwhelming, but it's not something beyond our grasp. Instead of allowing the sorrow of losing someone we love to engulf us, what if we could shift our perspective and see their departure not as an unbearable loss, but as a natural step in their soul's eternal journey? Yes, they may have been our "mother," "father," or someone we held so deeply in our hearts, but they, too, are beings evolving along their celestial path. It's a freeing thought, a gentle reminder that we all share the same inevitable destiny:

birth will eventually give way to death. When we open ourselves to this truth, the weight of our grief begins to soften, and in its place, we discover a quiet strength - a comforting peace that we are all part of something far greater than ourselves.

Reflecting on Smriti, Dhruv, and Aditi, one can't help but wonder how different their lives might have been if they had embraced a deeper understanding of life and death. If Smriti had believed that her mother's soul lived on beyond the physical world, perhaps her overwhelming grief would have softened, allowing her heart to heal in ways she couldn't imagine. And for Dhruv, a doctor driven by the desire to save lives, if he had understood that he couldn't control the outcome of every journey, perhaps he could have found some peace. Maybe he was meant to become a doctor to save many others, but not his mother's life - and in accepting this, he could have embraced the truth that each soul follows its own path, and death is an inevitable, natural part of that journey.

With this, I don't mean that adopting this perspective is simple - it's not. But I truly believe it can soften the weight of our grief, helping us find a way to live with less sorrow and more acceptance in the face of death.

जातस्य हि श्रुवो मृत्युर्श्वं जन्म मृतस्य च।
तस्मादपरिहार्येऽर्थ न त्वं शोचितुमरईसि॥ 2.27

{One who has taken his birth is sure to die, and after death one is sure to take birth again, Therefore, in the unavoidable discharge of your duty, you should not lament.}

अव्यक्तादीनि भूतानि व्यक्तमध्यानि भारत।
अव्यक्तनिधनान्येव तत्र का परिदेवना॥ 2.28

{All created beings are unmanifest in their beginning, manifest in their interim state, and unmanifest again when annihilated. So what need is there for lamentation?}

In the end, what we truly possess are the precious memories they left behind - their love, laughter, and the beauty of their life shared with us. We have the choice to hold onto these moments, reliving them with quiet joy, and letting their presence continue to warm our hearts. Rather than being weighed down by the ache of their absence, we can carry their spirit with us, finding comfort in the lasting imprint they've made on our lives.

DESTINY

Q23. Are we free to make desired choices or our lives are scripted?

There are times in life when we feel utterly lost, as if we're floating without direction, weighed down by helplessness, sorrow, and a deep confusion that clouds everything. The path ahead seems distant and unclear, and even the simplest decisions feel like towering cliffs, impossible to scale. It's not a rare moment, either. Life has a way of presenting these crossroad after crossroad, sometimes multiple times a day. Whether it's deciding on small, inconsequential things or making choices that alter the course of our lives, each decision, no matter how big or small, shapes who we are and who we become.

For children, the struggle begins with the small decisions - picking the perfect toy to play with, choosing between the red or blue shirt to wear, or deciding whether to spend the day playing outside in the fresh air or curled up inside with a favorite book. Even the simplest dilemma, like deciding whether to go to school or feigning a stomach ache to escape it, teaches them that choices are not as lighthearted as they seem; they carry meaning. But as teenagers, the weight of their choices grows heavier. Now, they stand at a crossroads, facing decisions that have the potential to shape their futures. Should they pursue what sets their hearts on fire, or yield to the quiet pressure of their parents' desires? Do they follow the subjects that ignite their curiosity, or opt for the ones that promise a more secure, practical future? It's a tug-of-war between their own dreams and the expectations placed upon them, each choice becoming a battle of identity and possibility.

A homemaker moves through her day in a world of constant choices, each one tethered to the well-being of her family. What meals will nourish them today, not just with food, but with love and care? Can she grant herself the small luxury of an afternoon nap to replenish her energy, or must she push through her exhaustion, putting everyone else's needs first? For those in the workforce, the experience is no less complex. The maze of competing priorities stretches on - should they devote themselves to climbing the career ladder, or carve out precious time for personal growth? Should they invest their energy in leading others, or focus on healing the relationships that have been neglected in the hustle of daily life? Every choice is a step forward, but it's also a moment that shapes the person we are becoming, leaving imprints on our hearts and minds.

In the Shadows of a Dream

Kartik, a grade ten student, standing on the precipice of his future, with a heart full of dreams and a mind clouded with doubt. The world around him seemed to be pulling in two directions: one led to the colorful, uncharted world of art that had always called to him, while the other stretched out before him like a well-lit, secure path, paved with the practicality of accounting. His parents, with their eyes set on stability, urged him toward a future that seemed safe, respectable, and predictable. They couldn't see what he saw - the bright hues of his dreams, the thrill of creating something from nothing. Instead, they saw the undeniable security in numbers and ledgers, and Kartik, too, bent to their vision, choosing spreadsheets over sketches.

It wasn't a decision made lightly. With every step he took in the direction of accounting, he left behind a piece of himself. He enrolled in the course, and while his classmates celebrated their first lessons in balance sheets, he tucked his love for art into the quiet corners of his heart, locked away. But that inner spark, the one that had once lit up his world with the vibrancy of creation, never completely faded.

Kartik's journey through school and college was a success by all outward measures. His report cards were filled with A's and distinctions, a clear reflection of his hard work and discipline. Yet beneath the surface, something was missing. The excitement of learning never quite touched him the way his art once had. The numbers he meticulously worked with neither painted the same depth nor meaning as the strokes of a brush on a canvas.

When he graduated and began searching for a job, the cracks in his perfect façade started to show. No matter how much he studied, no matter how many formulas he memorized, applying them in real-world scenarios felt foreign and exhausting. Job interviews were a maze of uncertainty, and each rejection gnawed at his confidence, reminding him of how far he had strayed from his true self. Despite his qualifications, he found himself trapped in a career he never wanted, one that brought no joy or fulfillment.

Years passed, and Kartik found himself sinking deeper into dissatisfaction. He had done everything he was supposed to do - excel in school, follow the path laid out for him - but something inside him remained unfulfilled. It wasn't until he hit rock bottom, after years of trying to fit into a mold that was never his, that he realized the truth: his heart had always been somewhere else.

One evening, overwhelmed with the weight of it all, Kartik reached for his old sketchbook. It was a relic from his childhood, pages filled with half-finished drawings and doodles that once brought him so much joy. At first, it was just a way to cope, a small act of rebellion against the life he had built. But soon, the simple act of sketching transformed him. It was like waking up from a long, painful sleep. His sketches were no longer just lines on paper; they were expressions of his soul, each stroke a small victory over the years of silence.

As he gained confidence, Kartik's passion grew. He took his sketchbook out into the world, capturing the faces of strangers in the bustling streets, in cafés, and even in quiet corners of restaurants. The modest income from these portraits wasn't much, but it was enough to remind him that he was capable of creating something real, something that came from the depths of his being. More importantly, it reignited his sense of purpose.

What started as pencil sketches soon evolved into digital art. His iPad became a portal to a new realm, a modern canvas that allowed him to explore and grow in ways he had never imagined. Graphic design, visual storytelling, and digital illustrations became his new playground, each medium unlocking more of his hidden potential. It was as though art had been waiting for him all along, and now, it was embracing him fully both, emotionally and financially.

Had he listened to his heart sooner, Kartik thought, perhaps he could have avoided those years of frustration. But his journey, though painful, had taught him that it is never too late to begin again. The power to reshape his destiny had always been within him; he just needed the courage to reach for it. Through the act of returning to his true passion, Kartik had learned that sometimes, the detours are just part of the path, and the most important step is the one we take to reclaim what we've lost.

*

In the Bhagavad Geeta, Lord Krishn delivers his most cherished and transformative lessons to Arjun guiding him through his doubts and moral struggles. After sharing the entirety of his teachings on the battlefield of the Kurukshetra - what we now know as "The Bhagavad Geeta" - Krishn entrusts Arjun with the freedom to choose his path. He places the power of decision firmly in Arjun's hands, encouraging him to reflect deeply on the wisdom imparted and decide for himself what action to take. This act of empowering Arjun underscores the profound respect Krishn holds for free will and personal responsibility in the journey of life.

Krishn offers Arjun the freedom to make his own decision, saying, "Thus, I have imparted to you the most confidential wisdom. Reflect on it thoroughly, and then act as you desire." This verse marks the conclusion of Krishn's teachings, emphasizing that wisdom is not something to be forced upon anyone, but rather something to be deeply contemplated and understood. It speaks to the essence of personal freedom in making choices, encouraging Arjun, and by extension all of us, to act from a place of personal reflection and inner realization. Ultimately, Krishn's guidance empowers Arjun to take responsibility for his actions, illustrating that true wisdom lies in the freedom to choose one's path after reflecting on the teachings received.

इति ते ज्ञानमाख्यातं गुह्याद्गुह्यतरं मया।
विमृश्यैतदशेषेण यथेच्छसि तथा कुरु॥ 18.63

{Thus, I have imparted to you the most confidential wisdom. Reflect on it thoroughly, and then act as you desire.}

This verse from the Bhagavad Geeta beautifully illustrates the depth of human freedom and the power of choice. After unveiling to Arjun the profound mysteries of existence and the essence of duty, Krishn does not impose a decision upon him. Instead, he places the responsibility squarely in Arjun's wish. With wisdom and compassion, Krishn equips Arjun with the understanding to discern right from wrong, yet he refrains from commanding a specific action. Arjun is left to wrestle with his own heart and conscience - to either rise as a warrior on the battlefield or walk away entirely as a coward. This moment is a poignant reminder that true guidance empowers rather than dictates.

This timeless truth teaches us that knowledge, no matter

how vast, is meaningless without action. It's a gentle reminder that our choices carry immense weight, shaping the course of our lives. Even God, with all His boundless wisdom, doesn't impose His will upon us - He honors our freedom to choose. Life becomes a delicate dance, a blend of destiny's quiet whispers and the bold steps of free will. It's in this interplay, between divine guidance and our own decisions, that the true beauty of our journey unfolds.

Many people willingly hand over their power of choice to the stars, convinced that life is entirely predestined. They pore over horoscopes, seeking guidance for even the tiniest decisions, as if their every move is already etched in an unchangeable script. While astrology can offer profound insights - much like a skilled doctor diagnosing an ailment - it's far from flawless. Predictions, no matter how precise, can miss the mark because life isn't a rigid blueprint. It's a fluid journey, shaped as much by the choices we make as by the circumstances we encounter.

The deeper truth lies in the law of karma. As we saw in Question 11, karma moves in ways that surpass human understanding, shaping our lives in ways no prediction ever could. It weaves our actions into the very essence of existence, reminding us that while fate may gently guide us down certain paths, it is the choices we make that truly shape our journey, giving us the power to define who we are along the way.

While that may have been a neutral perception, the truth is that even those burdened with the harshest and most challenging horoscopes can taste the sweetest nectar of life and beyond - by surrendering wholeheartedly at the feet of Krishn. For when He walks with you, what can truly go wrong?

Imagine life as a film, one where God is the director, and we are the actors, each of us stepping onto the stage of the world with roles to play of our lives. Our astrological charts are like the first draft of the script - an outline of who we are, where we might go, and what we might face. But the true beauty of the story lies in how we choose to play our parts. The universe isn't a rigid script; it's a living, breathing narrative, unfolding with every choice we make. Each decision, every action, breathes life into the plot, and with each moment, we have the chance to craft something deep, something meaningful.

The delicate balance between fate and free will is something we often misunderstand. When life is going well, we tend to take all the credit, basking in the glow of our hard work. But when things unravel, it's easy to point fingers at destiny, as though we had no part in it. Kartik's journey is a reminder of how flawed this thinking can be. Deep down, he always knew where his happiness laid, but for too long, he let others dictate the course of his life. Only when he finally embraced his own truth did the world around him begin to bloom with possibilities.

I'm a believer in astrology as well. Not only astrology but many other superpowers that exist above astrology. I do not defy the deep science of astrology. But I also believe in the magic that exists beyond it. Life isn't simply a matter of fate or pure free will - it's a beautiful, unpredictable dance between the paths the stars have set and the choices we carve for ourselves. There's a delicate balance, a harmony, between what is written in the heavens and the story we choose to create with our own hands. A beautiful tale from the Shrimad Bhagavata Mahapurana illustrates this very point.

When Devotion Defied Fate

There once lived a devotee, a simple man whose heart was entirely surrendered to Lord Krishn. He spent every moment of his life in worship, longing to meet his beloved Lord. One day, he encountered the great sage Narada on his wander and asked him, "Will I ever meet Lord Krishn? When will that happen? Will my devotion ever reach him?"

Narada, ever wise and aware of the ways of destiny, looked at the devotee and replied, "Your devotion is sincere, but according to the course of your destiny, you will need to continue your worship through many lifetimes (as many leaves on the tree behind him) before Krishn will reveal himself to you."

The devotee, instead of feeling discouraged, was filled with overwhelming joy. He thought to himself, If my devotion is reaching Krishn even now, then I am content - no matter how many lifetimes it takes! And with that realization, he began dancing with sheer bliss. His heart, flooded with gratitude, overflowed with the thought, How wonderful it is that God is listening to me, that my worship is being heard!

At that very moment, something miraculous occurred. Lord Krishn, moved by the depth of the devotee's emotion, appeared before him. The sight of Krishn, radiant and divine, overwhelmed the devotee, who could hardly believe his eyes. His joy knew no bounds.

However, Narada, who had witnessed this divine event, could not contain his frustration. Turning to Krishn, he said, "Lord, I spoke to this devotee truthfully, as you had told me. You said he would need many lifetimes of worship before meeting you. Yet here you are, appearing before him in this very lifetime! Have you not made me look like a fool?"

Krishn, with a serene smile, responded to Narada, his words carrying a deeper truth: "Narada, what I had told you was true - according to his destiny, this devotee was indeed meant to worship me through many lifetimes before meeting me. But what you did not understand is that the devotion he expressed, the deep, pure love so intense and so genuine that filled his heart at this moment - was supposed to reveal after a worship of many lifetimes but that it transcended his destined timeline. That very love, that overflow of emotion, brought me to him earlier than he could have foreseen."

He continued, "His worship was meant to evolve over many lifetimes, but in this lifetime, his soul's sentiment (bhaav), his heartfelt longing, reached me so powerfully that it called me here. It is not the number of lifetimes or the rituals that matter most; it is the sincerity of the heart, the depth of one's devotion, that draws me closer."

Narada, in awe of Krishn's words, bowed down, humbled by the boundless grace of the Lord. At that moment, he understood that devotion, when pure and true, has the power to transcend time and destiny itself.

*

This story of Narada and the devotee beautifully illustrates that even the destiny shaped by God's own hand can be transcended by the pure power of love, heartfelt actions, and unwavering devotion. It reminds us that while fate may set the course, the depths of our emotions, the sincerity of our choices, and the strength of our true sentiments can shift the very tides of our lives. When love is genuine and profound, it has the miraculous ability to defy even the most unyielding of destinies, revealing the extraordinary potential within us all to reshape our path.

Every decision we make leaves a mark, carving out the person we become, just as each action leaves a subtle impression on the canvas of our lives. Kartik's journey teaches us that even when we veer off course, we always have the chance to find our way back. Similarly, the devotee's unwavering love and pure devotion remind us that even destiny's script can be rewritten by the depth of our feelings and actions. If everything were solely destined, God would not have entrusted Arjun with the freedom to choose his path on the battlefield. The power to act, to change, and to redefine ourselves beyond the limits set by others or fate is the most precious gift we possess. In the end, we are not merely the product of fate; we are the architects of our own story, shaping our future with every step we take. What we choose, with sincerity and heartfelt devotion, ultimately defines who we are.

LIBERATION

Q24. How do I achieve liberation in the present life being surrounded by materialism?

Living in a world dominated by material pursuits, where our worth is often measured by wealth, accomplishments, and the fleeting highs of temporary pleasures - the idea of liberation can feel far out of reach. It's something that seems reserved for monks and mystics, people who have distanced themselves from the chaos of everyday life. But the true path to liberation isn't about escaping the world or abandoning our responsibilities. It's about learning how to move through life with a sense of freedom that comes from letting go of attachment and ego. It's about finding peace in the midst of the noise, transcending suffering not by withdrawing, but by engaging with life in a way that frees us from the grip of desire and fear. True liberation lies in being fully present in the world, yet not bound by it.

The answer lies in a shift within - how we think, how we act, how we react and how we connect with the world around us. The scriptures remind us that true liberation isn't about running away from the world, but about transforming the way we engage with it. It's about finding freedom in our hearts, where we cultivate inner detachment, letting go of the things that bind us. It's in mastering the art of selfless action, where we act not for ourselves, but for the greater good. And, most importantly, it's about realizing that everything we seek outside ourselves - the peace, the love, the fulfillment - is already there within us, waiting to be discovered.

The Cycle of Birth and Death: Breaking Free from Samsara

At the core of our existence, there beats a constant, unyielding rhythm - birth, death, and rebirth - a cycle we know as samsara. Life unfolds like a never-ending story, each chapter written by our desires, our attachments, and the choices we make. Every birth is colored by the echo of past actions, pulling us back into the world with the promise of unfinished lessons that still need to be learned. This cycle holds both a bittersweet beauty and a quiet sorrow: birth brings with it the hope and potential of new beginnings, but it also carries within it the certainty of endings. And with each ending comes the inevitable return of death, only to be followed by another birth, another chance to rise again. Yet, beneath this swirling dance of impermanence, there lies a deeper truth - we are bound in this cycle only until we awaken from the dream (illusion), breaking free from the endless loop of rebirth.

Our attachments to material pleasures, our identities, and the achievements we chase often feel like invisible chains, quietly binding us to the relentless cycle of existence. Desires are like seeds planted deep within our souls, and as long as they continue to grow - whether for love, wealth, or recognition - we remain tethered to the world, unable to break free. Yet, liberation, or moksha, is not found in rejecting life itself, but in transcending these desires. It's in learning to rise above the pull of what we crave, finding peace not by turning away from the world, but by seeing beyond it, allowing us to step out of the cycle and into the freedom that lies beyond attachment.

यं हि न व्यथयन्त्येते पुरुषं पुरुषर्षभ।
समदुःखसुखं धीरं सोऽमृतत्वाय कल्पते॥ 2.15

{O best among men [Arjun], the person who is not disturbed by happiness and distress and is steady in both is certainly eligible for liberation.}

Life, in all its complexity, inevitably brings us moments of joy and sorrow, of victory and defeat. We often find ourselves grasping tightly to the moments of happiness, unwilling to let go, while trying to push away the shadows of sorrow. This natural tendency traps us in an endless cycle of craving and disappointment, where joy slips through our fingers and pain lingers longer than it should. Yet, the truly wise understand this ultimate truth: liberation doesn't come from escaping life's inevitable ups and downs, but from finding balance within them. It's in cultivating equanimity - a peaceful steadiness of mind - that we begin to experience true freedom, learning to face both pleasure and pain without being swayed by either. This inner calm allows us to remain anchored, no matter how turbulent the storm.

This teaching reveals that true spiritual growth does not come from running away from life's ups and downs, but from learning to remain grounded despite them. It's about letting go of the constant pursuit of fleeting pleasures and the fear of inevitable hardships. When we stop clinging to these transient emotions, we free ourselves from the storm of turbulence that ties us to the material world. Equanimity offers a peaceful clarity, allowing us to view both joy and sorrow as passing moments - like seasons that change without leaving a trace on the soul. It's this inner calm, untouched by the surrounding chaos, that reveals the true freedom we seek.

The Role of Karma: Acting Without Attachment

Our actions are the building blocks of our journey, shaping every moment of our existence and guiding us through the endless cycle of birth and death. Every thought, word, and deed we put into the world leaves an imprint, creating echoes that reverberate through time and shape the experiences we are yet to face. It's a continuous cycle, each moment building on the next, with the weight of our choices guiding our path. Yet, the Bhagavad Geeta offers us a way out of this cycle - a path to liberation through karma yoga. This practice is the art of living with purpose and dedication, performing our actions with full presence, but without clinging to their results. It teaches us to surrender the fruits of our labor to God's feet, allowing us to find peace in the process rather than in the outcome. In this way, we free ourselves from the endless loop, and with each selfless act, we move closer to the freedom we seek.

बुद्धियुक्तो जहातीह उभे सुकृतदुष्कृते।
तस्माद्योगाय युज्यस्व योगः कर्मसु कौशलम्॥ 2.50

{A man engaged in devotional service rids himself of both good and bad actions even in this life. Therefore, strive for yoga, which is the art of all work.}

When we act without the desire for reward, we untangle the knots of karma that tie us to future births. A person who practices karma yoga does so with deep focus and devotion, yet without the weight of expectation hanging over them. They are like a parent who lovingly cares for their child, not seeking thanks or recognition, but simply offering their love. Or an artist, pouring their soul into their work, driven by the joy of creation rather than the pursuit of fame. In these moments, the act itself becomes a form of freedom - an expression of pure love and dedication, unburdened by the need for anything in return.

Liberation unfolds when we embrace life with an open heart, not burdened by expectations, but flowing with grace. It's in the simple act of letting go - releasing the need for recognition - that every moment transforms. Even the most ordinary tasks take on a sacredness, becoming offerings to the divine. This shift in perspective melts away the weight of both good and bad karma, clearing a path to true spiritual freedom. When we move through life with this purity of heart, we are no longer bound by the past or the future; we are free to simply be.

The world around us often leads us to believe that happiness can be found in the accumulation of things - more wealth, more achievements, more recognition. We chase after these fleeting rewards, thinking they will bring us lasting fulfillment. But true contentment isn't something that can be bought or earned. It comes from within, a quiet peace that remains untouched by the shifting tides of external circumstances. It is a deep, inner knowing that we are enough, exactly as we are, and that happiness isn't something we find, but something we create.

यदृच्छालाभसन्तुष्टो द्वन्द्वातीतो विमत्सरः।
समः सिद्धावसिद्धौ च कृत्वापि न निबध्यते॥ 4.22

{He who is satisfied with gain which comes of its own accord, who is free from duality and does not envy, who is steady in both success and failure, is never entangled, although performing actions.}

A truly wise person is not enslaved by possessions or recognition. They embrace both success and failure with a quiet grace, understanding that neither can define who they truly are. Their heart remains untouched by the ups and downs of life, for they know that true freedom doesn't lie in renouncing the world, but in living fully within it. True liberation arises not from abandoning all worldly roles but from performing them with an inner sense of freedom.

Transcending the Gunas: Escaping the Wheel of Rebirth

गुणानेतानतीत्य त्रीन्देही देहसमुद्भवान्।
जन्ममृत्युजरादुःखैर्विमुक्तोऽमृतमश्नुते॥ 14.20

{When the embodied being is able to transcend these three modes associated with the material body, he can become free from birth, death, old age, and their distresses and can enjoy nectar even in this life.}

Life operates under three modes, or *gunas*: sattva (goodness), rajas (passion), and tamas (ignorance). These forces shape our thoughts, actions, and emotions, pulling us back into the cycle of rebirth. Sattva may inspire peace, rajas drives ambition, and tamas induces inertia - but even these qualities are ultimately limitations.

Liberation involves transcending the influence of these gunas, moving beyond mental conditioning into a state of pure awareness. When we observe these modes without identifying with them, we loosen their grip over our consciousness. A person in this state sees the body and mind as instruments, knowing that the soul is eternal, beyond the fluctuations of life and death.

The Inner Awakening: Wisdom and Love

Through unwavering devotion and wisdom, the seeker aligns with the divine. This alignment purifies the heart, freeing it from attachments and misgivings. Liberation is not a destination but a state of being - where love, wisdom, and freedom flow effortlessly through every moment of life.

तद्बुद्धयस्तदात्मानस्तन्निष्ठास्तत्परायणाः।
गच्छन्त्यपुनरावृत्तिं ज्ञाननिर्धूतकल्मषाः॥ 5.17

{When one's intelligence, mind, faith, and refuge are all fixed in the Supreme, one becomes fully cleansed of misgivings through complete knowledge and thus proceeds straight on the path of liberation.}

तेषां सततयुक्तानां भजतां प्रीतिपूर्वकम्।
ददामि बुद्धियोगं तं येन मामुपयान्ति ते॥ 10.10

{To those who are constantly devoted to serving Me with love, I give the understanding by which they can come to Me.}

Thus, liberation is not an escape from life but an awakening to its deeper truth - a journey from the illusions of separation to the reality of unity. In this awakening, we rise above the cycle of birth and death, merging into the boundless, eternal flow of divine love, where we find peace in oneness.

The Path of Surrender

मन्मना भव मद्भक्तो मद्याजी मां नमस्कुरु।
मामेवैष्यसि सत्यं ते प्रतिजाने प्रियोऽसि मे॥ 18.65

{Always think of Me, become My devotee, worship Me, and offer your homage unto Me. Thus you will come to Me without fail, I promise you this because you are My very dear friend.}

Surrendering to the divine is not about giving up but about trusting in a higher purpose. It is an invitation to release the illusion of control and let the divine guide our actions. This trust allows us to live fully without fear, knowing that we are part of a greater whole. As it says:

"सर्वधर्मान्परित्यज्य" - does not imply the rejection of all other religions (in reference to duties and doubts) in existence. Instead, this verse calls upon us to let go of doubts, fears, and attachments to worldly desires - the chains that bind the soul. It conveys to free ourselves from these distractions and align our hearts with divine truth.

"मामेकं शरणं व्रज" - surrender fully to the one and only Krishn. This surrender can take many devotional forms, but the most tangible and accessible in this material world is through his divine name (chanting his name) - as suggested in the last chapter of the Bhagavat Purana to be the most simply effective savior in Kaliyug. By immersing yourself in the repetition of Krishn's sacred name, you transcend the chaos of the external world and awaken to the divine. It is a practice where the self dissolves, and only the name remains - guiding, uplifting, and ultimately liberating.

"अहं त्वा सर्वपापेभ्यो मोक्षयिष्यामि मा शुचः" - In these words, Krishn offers an extraordinary promise, a divine assurance that He Himself will liberate us from all sins and burdens. There is no condition too great, no past too tainted for His grace. He gently calls us to surrender completely, without reservation or hesitation, trusting in His infinite compassion.

This verse is not merely a promise; it is a refuge. Krishn asks us to come to Him wholeheartedly, leaving behind our fears, doubts, and regrets. In His shelter, there is no room for guilt or anxiety - only the peace of knowing that divine love will dissolve every mistake. When we abandon our ego and lean into this trust, liberation is not just a distant goal but a living reality. His promise through these words unburdens our hearts, reminding us that in surrender, we gain everything, and in His embrace, fear ceases to exist.

When we surrender, we dissolve the ego - the false sense of separation that keeps us bound to samsara. In surrender, we no longer act from fear or desire but from a place of love and trust. This act of surrender liberates us from the endless cycles of birth and death, bringing us closer to the divine essence within.

सर्वधर्मान्परित्यज्य मामेकं शरणं व्रज।
अहं त्वा सर्वपापेभ्यो मोक्षयिष्यामि मा शुचः॥ 18.66

{Abandon all varieties of religion and just surrender unto Me. I shall deliver you from all sinful reactions. Do not fear.}

GLOSSARY

1. **Bhagavad Gita:** A timeless spiritual guide that forms part of the *Mahabharata*, where Lord Krishna shares profound teachings with Arjuna on the battlefield of Kurukshetra. It addresses life, duty, and the path to self-realization, offering insights into how one can live a righteous, peaceful life.
2. **Saptadashi:** Derived from the Sanskrit word for seventeen, it refers to the 17 significant themes explored in this book, each drawn from the *Bhagavad Gita*, offering timeless wisdom relevant to our modern lives.
3. **Karma:** The law of action and consequence. Every action, thought, or intention we have influences the world around us and shapes our future. The idea is to act with awareness and righteousness, knowing that every act creates a ripple effect in our lives.
4. **Svarupa:** This refers to one's true, unchanging nature. It's the essence of who we are beyond the body, mind, and ego. Realizing our svarupa is the ultimate goal of self-awareness.
5. **Maya:** The illusion of the material world. It is the divine force that causes the soul to forget its true nature and become absorbed in the fleeting reality of the material world. Maya makes us believe in the

reality of things that are temporary and ever-changing.

6. **Atman:** The individual soul or self, which is eternal and beyond the physical body. Atman is part of the universal divine, pure and unchanging, and is one with the Supreme Soul in its purest form.
7. **Brahman:** The Supreme, all-encompassing reality. It is formless, infinite, and the source of all creation, permeating every part of the universe and existing beyond space and time.
8. **Bhakti:** The path of devotion and love for the Divine. Bhakti involves surrendering to God with full faith, love, and trust. It's about cultivating a personal relationship with the Divine, where every act becomes an offering of love.
9. **Yoga:** More than just physical exercises, yoga is a spiritual practice that aims to unite the individual soul (Atman) with the Supreme (Brahman). There are different paths of yoga, such as Karma Yoga (the yoga of action), Bhakti Yoga (the yoga of devotion), and Jnana Yoga (the yoga of knowledge).
10. **Samsara:** The continuous cycle of birth, death, and rebirth. It's the wheel of life that keeps the soul trapped in the material world until it attains liberation.
11. **Moksha:** Liberation or freedom from the cycle of samsara. It's the state of pure consciousness, free

from attachment and ego, where the soul experiences unity with the Divine.

12. **Gunas:** The three fundamental qualities of nature that influence human behavior and the material world: Sattva (purity and goodness), Rajas (passion and activity), and Tamas (ignorance and inertia). These modes affect how we think, feel, and act in the world.
13. **Jnana:** Knowledge, especially spiritual wisdom, that leads to a deeper understanding of the self and the world. It's not just intellectual knowledge but experiential realization that connects the individual with the Divine.
14. **Dharma:** Righteous duty or the moral path. It refers to the ethical and spiritual responsibilities we have, based on our role in society and life. Dharma is the guiding principle that helps us live in harmony with the world and our true self.
15. **Detachment:** The practice of not being attached to the results of actions or material possessions. It doesn't mean renouncing the world but acting without selfish desires, allowing one to stay peaceful, regardless of external outcomes.
16. **Arjuna:** The central figure in the *Bhagavad Gita*, a warrior prince caught in a moral and spiritual crisis on the battlefield. His conversation with Krishna forms the foundation of the teachings, as he seeks guidance on duty, life, and his purpose.

17. **Krishna:** The Supreme Lord in the *Bhagavad Gita*, who appears as Arjuna's charioteer and spiritual guide. Krishna represents divine wisdom, love, and the ultimate truth, teaching Arjuna - and all of us - how to live a life of purpose, devotion, and balance.
18. **Vairagya:** Renunciation or detachment from the material world. It is the state of being free from desires and attachments, enabling one to focus on spiritual growth and realize their true nature.
19. **Sankhya:** A school of philosophy that emphasizes knowledge and understanding of the self as the path to liberation. Sankhya teaches that by realizing the distinction between the eternal soul and the changing material world, one can attain freedom.
20. **Prakriti:** Nature or the material world, which is made up of the three gunas. It is the dynamic force that creates and sustains the universe, often seen as the "playground" where souls undergo their journey in samsara.
21. **Raja Yoga:** The yoga of meditation and mind control. It involves practices to calm the mind, reach inner stillness, and realize one's true nature. It is the path of discipline and spiritual focus.
22. **Sadhana:** The spiritual practice or discipline undertaken to achieve a specific goal, often in the context of attaining self-realization or devotion to the Divine. It's a personal journey of growth through dedication and effort.

23. **Ahankara (Ego):** The sense of "I" or "me," often associated with the ego. The false sense of self, created by attachment to the body and mind. It is the part of us that identifies with the material world and separates us from our true nature. Overcoming ego is essential for spiritual growth.
24. **Tapas:** Spiritual discipline or austerity that purifies the mind and body. It's about dedicating oneself to practices like meditation, fasting, and self-restraint in order to overcome distractions and progress on the spiritual path.
25. **Sharanagati (Surrender):** The act of surrendering oneself completely to the Divine will. It is the path of total trust and devotion, where one lets go of the ego and allows God's guidance to lead them toward liberation.
26. **Ananda:** Bliss or eternal happiness that comes from realizing the oneness with the Divine. It is the natural state of the soul when it is freed from the confines of ego and illusion.
27. **Mantra:** A sacred sound, word, or phrase repeated in meditation to focus the mind and connect with the divine. Mantras are tools for spiritual growth and can help quiet the mind and elevate the consciousness.
28. **Kshetra:** Literally, "field," referring to the body and mind as the "field" of experience in which the soul (Kshetragna) interacts with the material world. The

field is where one's actions take place and spiritual progress is made.

29. **Vishnu:** One of the principal deities in Hinduism, often seen as the preserver and protector of the universe. In the *Bhagavad Gita*, Krishna is considered an incarnation of Vishnu.
30. **Satya:** Truth; the ultimate reality or absolute truth that transcends the material world. Satya is one of the values that guide ethical living and spiritual practice.
31. **Bhava:** Feeling, mood, or state of being. In the context of devotion, it refers to the attitude or emotional state of the devotee toward the Divine, such as love, reverence, or longing.
32. **Tattva:** Truth or principle. It refers to the ultimate reality or essence of things. Tattva is often discussed in spiritual texts as the nature of the self, the universe, and the Supreme.
33. **Yajna:** A sacrificial ritual or offering to the Divine. It is an act of selfless service and devotion, where material offerings are made to achieve spiritual benefits and cosmic harmony.
34. **Shakti:** Power or energy, often associated with the feminine aspect of the Divine. Shakti represents the dynamic force that creates and sustains the universe, often personified as the goddess.
35. **Santosha:** Contentment or inner peace. It refers to the state of being satisfied with what one has, free

from desire or dissatisfaction, and is an important aspect of spiritual well-being.

36. **Sadhu:** A holy person or saint; an individual who has devoted themselves to spiritual practice and lives a life of simplicity and virtue. A sādhu is respected for their wisdom and dedication.
37. **Kshetragna:** The "knower of the field," referring to the soul, which is the eternal observer of the body and mind (the "field"). The soul is distinct from the material body and its activities.
38. **Pranayama:** Breath control; a series of techniques used in yoga to regulate the breath, calm the mind, and increase spiritual awareness. Pranayama is believed to purify the body and mind.
39. **Rupa:** Form or shape. In a spiritual context, it refers to the divine form or manifestation of the Supreme. Lord Krishna is often described as having a divine *rupa*, beyond human comprehension.
40. **Sankalpa:** Intention or resolve. It is the mental commitment to pursue a specific goal, especially on the spiritual path. Sankalpa is a powerful force that directs one's actions and thoughts.
41. **Anitya:** Impermanence or the transient nature of all things in the material world. The concept of anitya emphasizes that everything in the physical realm is temporary and subject to change.
42. **Chitta:** The mind or consciousness. Chitta encompasses all aspects of the mind, including

thoughts, emotions, and memories. In spiritual practice, controlling and purifying the chitta is essential for self-realization.

43. **Avidya:** Ignorance or the lack of true knowledge. Avidya is the root cause of the illusion of separation and the soul's entanglement in the material world. Overcoming avidya is central to spiritual awakening.
44. **Vishvarupa:** The universal form of the Divine, often depicted as the all-encompassing cosmic vision shown by Krishna to Arjuna in the *Bhagavad Gita*. It reveals the vastness of God's presence in the universe.
45. **Karma Yoga:** The path of selfless action, where one acts without attachment to the results. It involves doing one's duty with love and dedication, offering the fruits of actions to the Divine.
46. **Jnana Yoga:** The path of knowledge and wisdom, where one seeks to understand the nature of the self and the universe. It is the pursuit of truth through self-inquiry and intellectual understanding.
47. **Dhyana:** Meditation or focused contemplation. Dhyana is the practice of quieting the mind, concentrating on a single point of focus, and ultimately realizing one's true nature.
48. **Shanti:** Peace, tranquility, or calm. Shanti is often invoked in prayers and mantras as a state of inner harmony and spiritual balance.

49. **Tula:** Balance or equilibrium. In spiritual terms, tula represents the harmonious state of mind where one is free from extremes and has found inner peace.
50. **Lila:** Divine play or the playful activity of the Supreme Lord. Lila refers to the belief that the universe and all creation are an expression of God's playful will, and that everything is part of a divine, joyful purpose.
51. **Pratibimba:** Reflection; often used to describe the material world as a reflection of the divine reality. The material universe is seen as a mirror of the transcendental.
52. **Aham Brahmasmi:** "I am Brahman"—a famous Vedantic saying that expresses the realization of one's identity with the ultimate reality, Brahman. It represents the state of self-awareness where the individual soul recognizes itself as one with the Supreme.
53. **Siddhi:** Spiritual accomplishment. Siddhis are extraordinary powers or abilities attained through intense spiritual practice. They are seen as by-products of spiritual discipline, not the goal of practice itself.

REFERENCES

Annual Review of Neuroscience. 2022. "Breathing Rhythm and Pattern and Their Influence on Emotion." Annual Reviews. Breathing Rhythm and Pattern and Their Influence on Emotion.

Chaube, R. K., V. K. Chaube, P. Saxena, K. Solanki, RVC Tiwari, and H. Tiwari. 2020. "Scientific rationale of Yagya: a review." International Journal of Community Medicine and Public Health. https://behindeverytemple.org/wp-content/uploads/2022/02/Scientific_rationale_of_Yagya_a_review.pdf.

Das, Subhendu. 2020. "Yogic Power -The Highest Power in Nature." ResearchGate. https://www.researchgate.net/publication/346579408_Yogic_Power_-The_Highest_Power_in_Nature.

Doniger, Wendy. 1998. "Vedic religion | Origins, Beliefs & Practices." Britannica. https://www.britannica.com/topic/Vedic-religion.

Goenka, SN. n.d. "S. N. Goenka." Vipassana Research Institute. https://www.vridhamma.org/S.N.-

Goenka?utm_source=chatgpt.com#EarlyYears.

"How Agnihotra saved a family from Bhopal Gas Tragedy ?" 2012. Hindu Janajagruti Samiti. https://www.hindujagruti.org/news/15349.html.

McGreevey, Sue. 2013. "Mind-body Genomics." Harvard Edu. https://hms.harvard.edu/news/mind-body-genomics?utm_source=chatgpt.com.

Nayan, Nishant. 2023. "Pind Daan In Gaya - Analyzing Its Importance In Hindu Way Of Life Through The Ancient Texts." *Journal of Research in Humanities and Social Science* 11, no. 9 (September): 118-123. https://www.questjournals.org/jrhss/papers/vol11-issue9/1109118123.pdf?utm_source=chatgpt.com.

Rao, Rekha. 2024. "Putrakameshti Yajna and the Birth of Rama." Indica.in. https://www.indica.today/quick-reads/utrakameshti-yajna-and-birth-of-rama-in-ramayana/.

Reddy, MS. 2012. "Psychotherapy - Insights from Bhagavad Geeta - PMC." PubMed Central. https://pmc.ncbi.nlm.nih.gov/articles/PMC3361835/.

S, Verma, Mishra A, and Shrivastava V. 2018.

"Yagya Therapy in Vedic and Ayurvedic Literature: A Preliminary exploration." Interdisciplinary Journal of Yagya Research. https://doi.org/10.36018/ijyr.v1i1.7.

"Temple Architecture – Devalaya Vastu – Part Five (5 of 9)." 2012. sreenivasarao's blogs. https://sreenivasaraos.com/2012/09/09/temple-architecture-devalaya-vastu-part-five-5-of-7/.

Times of India. 2024. "What is Pran Pratistha and why the Shankracharyas are not attending it." *Times of India*, January 15, 2024. https://timesofindia.indiatimes.com/life-style/soul-search/what-is-pran-pratistha-and-why-the-shankracharyas-are-not-attending-it/photostory/106862426.cms.

Warren, Shellie R. 2024. "How energy exchange during sex affects you and your vibe." xonecole. https://www.xonecole.com/end-of-the-year-checklist/.

ACKNOWLEDGMENTS

My heartfelt gratitude goes to Dr. Mihir Upadhyay, my esteemed Sanskrit Guru, whose unwavering faith in me has been a constant source of strength. Under his guidance, I've had the privilege of diving into the original texts of Indian scriptures, uncovering their true meanings while avoiding the confines of jargon. More than a teacher, he has been a mentor who saw potential in me I hadn't yet discovered.

I am deeply thankful to my Guruji Dr. Shreedhar Santananbhai Vyas, the "Krishn to my Arjun," for empowering me to see this project through to completion. His wisdom, rooted in the sacred traditions of India, has been invaluable. I will always be grateful for his encouragement and for the spontaneous title he gave to this book - a title that perfectly encapsulates its essence. His wisdom is a guiding light that continues to inspire me beyond words. I wholeheartedly believe that without the guidance of my teachers, I would not be the woman I am today.

Besides my formal teachers, I am forever indebted to my first Guru, my beloved mother, who nurtured my love for mythology even before I was born. Her stories from the scriptures and the sacred conversations we shared filled my heart with a deep connection to the divine. It is through her that I first glimpsed the beauty and wisdom of these ancient texts, and for that, I am eternally grateful.

Furthermore, I wish to acknowledge the English translations of the Bhagavat Gita verses are sourced from *Bhagavad-Geeta As It Is* by His Divine Grace A.C. Bhaktivedanta Swami Prabhupada, whose work has guided many on their spiritual journeys. While, the English translations of verses from *Shrimad Bhagavata Mahapurana* are sourced from Bhagavata.org, a valuable resource preserving the wisdom of this sacred text.

Lastly, I fully acknowledge that there may be errors in this book, Whether through misattributing ideas or neglecting to give credit where it is due. Any such oversight is unintentional, and I deeply regret any omissions or inaccuracies.

www.ingramcontent.com/pod-product-compliance
Lightning Source LLC
LaVergne TN
LVHW091252150826
845673LV00006B/1393

* 9 7 8 9 3 3 4 0 5 9 4 0 3 *